JOURNEY TO THE TOP LOT

God's GRAND PLAN on His Holy Mountain of Faith

LESLEY MASON VAITEKUNAS OFS

SILVERSMITH
PRESS

Published by Silversmith Press—Houston, Texas
www.silversmithpress.com

Copyright © 2024 Lesley Mason Vaitekunas OFS

All rights reserved.

This book, or parts thereof, may not be reproduced in any form or by any means without written permission from the publisher, except for brief passages for purposes of reviews.

The views and opinions expressed here in belong to the author and do not necessarily represent those of the publisher.

ISBN 978-1-961093-49-2 (Softcover Book)
ISBN 978-1-961093-50-8 (eBook)

To God be all the glory!

The Lord says, "I will teach you the way you should go;
I will instruct you and advise you."
Psalms 32.8

CONTENTS

Preface vii

Part I

1: A Birth before the Sunrise 3
2: My Parents "Bought the Farm" 7
3: My Very Independent Nature 10
4: More Childhood Memories 12
5: Auntie FranCies 18
6: My Love for the "Top Lot" And For God Begins 22
7: And Now a Little More About Our "Pa" 25
8: Ouch! And Some Happy Memories Too 28
9: The Fun and the Sad Times of Life on the Farm 32
10: My Wonderful Ma "This too shall pass." 38
11: B.M. in the A.M. Grandpa Comes to Live With Us 42
12: A Bad and a Good Year for Me 44
13: Snow and Freezing Cold Experiences as a Teen 46
14: Exchange Student Experiences 50
15: Graduation from High School and
     My Nursing School Experiences 54
16: Country Girls Move to the BIG CITY! 59
17: Three Nurses in an M.G. Midget on a Trip to Florida ... 63
18: Working in the Emergency Department 66
19: Adoption of My Beautiful Baby Daughter 80
20: My "Forever Husband" 86
21: A Glass of Ice Water!
     The Beginning of My Conversion to the Catholic Faith ... 88
22: Conversion of a Very Protesting Protestant
     Into the Catholic Faith 95
23: How I Came to Believe In the In the Most Holy Eucharist ... 98
24: My Entrance into
     the Catholic Church and My Life's Mission 101

25: The "Top Lot" is God's Holy Mountain of Faith 105
26: Spiritual Warfare and Intercessory Prayer
    The Good and the Bad 112
27: The Sonlight Clown Ministry 114
28: The Meeting of a Holy Carmelite priest 121
29: A Meeting with the Bishop 130
30: PRAYING FOR OUR PRIESTS 132
31: "You are the GOD MOTHER of ALL priests." 136
32: Experiences with Different priests over the Years 138
33: More GODcidences 142
34: A Priest from Nigeria and His First Night in America
    And Other Experiences With Nigerian priests 144
35: My Mission in Life
    The "Top Lot" Ministry for priests 149

Part II
Talks Given Over the Years

36: Saint Pio of Pietrelcina, Capuchin
    "Our Go-To" Saint For The Top Lot!" 153
37: THE "BUILDING" OF A PRIEST AND PERSEVERANCE 160
38: "A priest goes to Heaven or a priest goes to Hell
    with a thousand people behind." 163
39: The Lives of the Saints 165
40: Some Things I Have "Heard In My Heart" 167
41: FAITH AND ENDURANCE A Talk for the Youth of Our Church 169
42: Sanctification of the Present Moment 8/2/02 2:44 a.m. (LV)
    Or "Living In the Here and NOW!" Not Our Way, Not Our Will 181
43: "Be Yea Fishers of Men"
    A Talk for the Youth Group Summer Retreat 2005 192
44: Talks For the "Army of God" Intercessory Prayer Group 198
45: How to Prepare For Intercessory Prayer Or
    Rather How to Allow HIM to Prepare You 202
46: KEEP YOUR EYES ON JESUS 205
47: HOLINESS 210
48: The Eucharist
    A Talk Given to the Youth on Dec. 10, 2002 216
49: Eucharistic Miracles 223
50: Scriptural Basis of the Eucharist 226
51: Our Lives Are Like A Stream In the Desert (LV) 229
52: "Gramma Rosa"
    The Power of Prayer, Even in the Little Things 231
53: Some DAILY PRAYERS You Might Like 233

PREFACE

Forgive me Lord.

For several years I have sensed "nudgings" to write a book of my story, my testimony. And several have told me I need to write a book. However, I have always "pushed these aside" with thoughts like, "Who am I to write a book?" Indeed, "Who am I to write a book?" I am a child of God, created by Him, and made in His image to give Him ALL THE GLORY. I hope to do so through this book, it is not a book about ME; it is a book about HIM!

I would like to ask the Lord's forgiveness. "Forgive me Lord for pushing You aside for so long. How often have I "pushed You aside?" But You have never left me, You have never "pushed me aside" over the course of my life. Thank You, Jesus, for always "being there" for me. Now, I ask You to always help me to be there for You, to do Your Will.

Aren't we all guilty of "pushing God away" when we do not want to do what He wants us to do? Help us Lord to embrace You and embrace Your Cross instead of resisting You, instead of pushing You aside.

Forgive me Lord for the times I did not move forward with writing a book the first time You "nudged" me back in 1991, then in 1995, 2005, again in 2007. These were all attempts when I started writing my book but never kept going, never finishing. This time, in 2024, I FINISHED MY BOOK with YOUR help. Thank You, Lord!

I also want to take this opportunity to give thanks to God for my husband, Matt. For Mother's Day this year, 2023, he connected me up with a publisher, Joanna Hunt with Silversmith Publishing, "Publish and Go." She has been a great help in teaching me how to write this book. So I have FINALLY written my book! It is all about what GOD has done in my life. I also want to give thanks to all my friends, priests, and lay people, who have supported me through their prayers.

PART I

1
A BIRTH BEFORE THE SUNRISE

I was born on April 3rd, 1948, in the Community Hospital in Stamford, New York, which no longer exists. I was told I came into the world early in the morning, before the sunrise, and in time for my "PA" to return to do the chores, that of milking the cows and all the other things a farmer must do.

My parents were two American Baptists. I was born into a family with two older brothers.

My Father, (A.K.A. "Pa") named me Lesley, after a poem written by his favorite Scottish poet, Robert Burns. It was called "Bonnie Lesley." He used to read it to me with a Scottish accent. My Mother (A.K.A. "Ma") was of Scottish descent.

JOURNEY TO THE TOP LOT

Bonnie Lesley

O SAW ye bonnie Lesley
As she gaed o'er the Border?
She's gane, like Alexander,
To spread her conquests farther.

To see her is to love her,
And love but her forever;
For Nature made her what she is,
And ne'er made anither!

Thou art a queen, fair Lesley,
Thy subjects we, before thee:
Thou art divine, fair Lesley,
The hearts o' men adore thee.

The Deil he couldna scaith thee,
Or aught that wad belang thee;
He'd look into thy bonnie face
And say, 'I canna wrang thee!'

*The Powers aboon will tent thee,
Misfortune sha'na steer thee:
Thou'rt like themsel' sae lovely,
That ill they'll ne'er let near thee.

Return again, fair Lesley,
Return to Caledonie!
That we may brag we hae a lass
There's nane again sae bonnie!

4

1: A BIRTH BEFORE THE SUNRISE

And the *"powers above"* did protect me all throughout my life.

At the age of six months, according to my "Ma" I almost died. My "Pa" used to have young men attending high school in NYC come to the farm in the summer to help with the haying. I was in my playpen out on the porch of the farmhouse. One of the hired hands came in and bent down to play with me. Shortly thereafter I started choking. My parents took me to the old "Doc" in a town eleven miles from the farm. He looked and looked in my mouth and throat but could not see anything, so home I went.

But I was still coughing. Finally, my "Ma" saw what the problem was; evidently when the hired hand bent over to play with me, he had a piece of "timothy" hay in his pant leg. I must have grabbed it without him being aware of it. Timothy has barbs on the end of it, and this is what was stuck in my throat. While choking and crying, my "Ma" saw the problem. After a second trip to the Doc, he was finally able to remove the "timothy" with a pair of forceps, thus saving my life. So I guess God surely had future plans for me.

He has plans for your life too. Ask Him what He wants you to do with your life. Over time, He will let you know in many ways.

If God can use me, a little farm girl from Upstate New York, for His "GREATER PURPOSE," He can use anyone. All you must do is pray and ask HIM to show YOU what HE wants YOU to do. PERSEVERE and never give up! He will show you HIS WILL in your life, whatever that may be. I will pray for all those who read this book and beg you to please pray for God's "Grand Plan" (more about that later!) to be completed in His time. AMEN.

2
MY PARENTS "BOUGHT THE FARM"

Pa grew up in New York City, so he was a "city boy." When he was an adult, he owned his own printing business. He became ill from lead poisoning, and the doctor told him, "You have to sell your business and move to the country and drink lots of milk."

He did not know anything about farming, but he was a smart guy. He went to the library in NYC and took notes on how to farm. The only place he knew in the country was a Boy's Camp where he had worked as a teen. He purchased a 176-acre farm for $2,400, and that included lots of farm equipment and sixteen cows. The farm is also on a beautiful lake. He bought it all from an elderly spinster lady we called "Auntie FranCies." She is the lady who ran the boy's camp when he was a teen. She was not a blood relative, but out of respect, we had to call everyone aunt or uncle.

My parents had to allow her to continue to run her summer business down by the lake and to allow her to live in part of our farmhouse until she passed to eternal life. She lived to be ninety-eight. She had four cabins she rented to city people for the summer. The husbands worked in New York City, and the wives and kids would stay in the country. The husbands would drive to the country over the weekends to be with their families. (The "boys camp" had closed after the stock market crash in 1929.)

She had three upstairs rooms in our farmhouse and two downstairs rooms where she lived with her cats, more about them and her later.

My parents moved from NYC to the farm in upstate NY in November 1941, about a month before the Pearl Harbor attack, that occurred on December 7, 1941. They brought their firstborn, my brother, Bill, with them. One day my ma accidentally dropped his wet diaper on the floor. Family lore tells us it was so cold in the old farmhouse that two seconds later the diaper froze to the floor.

The first summer my pa was on the farm he cut a twenty-plus acre hay field with a handheld scythe, all by himself. The next year the local farmers helped him and taught him how to be a farmer. They all helped each other during haying or putting silage into the silo. It would become neighbor helping neighbor for years to come.

My other brother, Don, was born shortly before the atom bomb was dropped on Hiroshima on August 6th, 1945, and then the other one three days later on Nagasaki.

During WWII my ma had to be frugal with her cooking. One funny story they told was when she made a salad with chopped up grass in it. However, one of the grass pieces

2: MY PARENTS "BOUGHT THE FARM"

was not chopped up small enough. My oldest brother said, "Ma there is GRASS in this salad!" This story has been passed down from generation to generation.

My parents knew several married couples, who were also farmers, and they would play pinochle together. They took turns meeting at different homes once a month. When they were at our house, I remember my bedroom was right above where they would play cards. I used to put my ear to the floor register, a vent allowing heat to rise upstairs, and I had a grand old time listening to all the talk/gossip going on down below in the living room. One night a bat had flown down from the chimney and all the women were screaming and running around. Quite a memorable occasion!

And that reminds me of another "bat story." One day there was a bat in the kitchen. My ma got a dish towel and threw it over the bat and took it outside and shook it. She then returned to the house and put the dish towel down on the table. After a few minutes, the towel started to move across the table. It seems ma shook it outside, but the bat hung on tight!

I guess having bats in the attic is better than having bats in the belfry. It seems the lesson from this chapter would be perseverance, both for my parents and for the bat. Always remember to hang on tight and enjoy the ride no matter how bumpy/batty the road may be.

3

MY VERY INDEPENDENT NATURE

One day, at the age of three, I was lost. My parents seldom left me, but that day Auntie FranCies had the task of watching me. She called out to me, "Lesley, where are you?" She searched and searched, all to no avail. We lived very close to a lake, so I am sure she was frantic. She kept yelling, "Lesley, where are you?" She was quite angry when she came upon "Little Lesley" (me!) sitting in the middle of a big pile of hay in the barn. She asked me, "Didn't you hear me? Why didn't you answer me when I called you?"

I responded, "Yes, I heard you; well, I knew where I was!" This showed my very independent nature from a very early age.

This example of "Little Lesley" enjoying being alone became a very common thread in the tapestry of my life. I was quite independent and loved to be alone. This independent nature was both an asset and a detriment at times in my life.

3: MY VERY INDEPENDENT NATURE

Living in the country gave me many opportunities to hide. Another favorite hiding place was in the kitchen wood box. I loved to try to scare my brothers when they would return from school.

Out behind the farmhouse was a road climbing up a steep hill, a road later named after my parents. On one side of the hill was a very secluded area with a huge rock and lots of flowers. I used to hide there in my little haven of peace and quiet and watch the world go by, which consisted of a very occasional car passing by.

Another favorite spot was on a large rock surrounded by tall grass. No one could see me, and I used to love to sit on that rock and enjoy myself thinking that no one knew where I was. Great fun for a little girl!

We used to have a sunflower patch, and at the age of three or four I loved to sit out among the sunflowers. I loved to be alone so I could think and be quiet, even at that young age.

Sometimes I would go up in the haymow of the barn just to watch through the cracks in the wood slats to see if anyone came down the road. Another fun activity was hanging on a rope from a high beam in the haymow and swinging into the huge pile of hay. Of course, that was before they had hay bales!

Do you like to be alone? Being alone with God is a great gift! Take time to be alone with Him, and don't forget to take time to smell the flowers too! To God be all the Glory!

4
MORE CHILDHOOD MEMORIES

When I was three or four, we all went to the drive-in theatre in our car. I sat on the floor in the front seat, and I somehow kicked the emergency brake off, and the car rolled backward and ripped out the speaker. Thankfully it didn't break the window. Pa moved the car to another spot, and the movie viewing continued. He turned in the speaker as he drove away after the movie. I don't recall us ever going to the movies again! Wonder why?

In kindergarten, one day after I returned home, I told my ma a story. I said, "Someone broke a glass milk bottle at school today."

She asked me more about it, and I said, "Yes, someone broke it, and I spilled milk all over the floor!" Of course, that "someone" was me!

I used to love making mud pies out near our clothesline. Ma could watch me from the kitchen window as I played making my pies. Of course, I thought I was a big girl as

4: MORE CHILDHOOD MEMORIES

I was out there all by myself as I was "baking" in my make-believe world.

When I was four my brother Don used to play tea-time with me. We sat outside at a little table, and I had the grandest fun. He watched over me a lot when I was very young. Of course, as a teenager, he used to tease me like most brothers do.

At about five years old, our closest neighbor brought his horse over one day, and I had my first experience with a horse. It gave me a love for horses at a very young age. More about my own horse later.

I also remember my first hair permanent at the age of eight. I think my city grandmother influenced my ma to have it done. I think Grandma was trying to turn me into a "girly girl!" O' how I hated that permanent and could not wait till it grew out. Growing up on a farm with two older brothers made me a bit of a "tomboy," and I did not like this new look.

One of my favorite memories is the time my oldest brother, Bill, came home from college. My brothers had a contest each year with the neighborhood boys as they would come over to our farm and "steal" their Christmas tree from us, and we would do the same on their property. It was a Christmas tradition.

So, my brothers and I went over to the neighbor's farm, and they cut down our Christmas tree. After we had cut our tree, we had to carry it across the frozen lake. I felt so important when they allowed me to "help them" by carrying the top part of the tree, which of course was the lightest part. It sure made me feel important to know I helped!

We had lots of fun memories on that lake in the winter. We would ice skate, and the boys would play hockey. I remember the lake making loud booming noises on occasion. That was a little scary for me. But it was a natural phenomenon caused by ice expansion.

In the spring when the ice started to melt, my brothers and the same neighborhood boys had a competition each year as to who would jump into the lake first. Of course, I always thought my brothers won the contest. I wasn't a fool enough to participate in such craziness.

A summer memory was when I was with my brothers out in a field. One of my brothers smoked a cigarette. I was appalled! They swore me to secrecy, and I never told anyone, until now! However, because of this incident, they gave me my nickname. It was smoke click, thistle foot, then they added the name of a boy that I did not like and ended it with a boy that I did like by saying he loved another girl in my class. They would say it in a teasing manner, sometimes even singing it to me. I would cry whenever they teased me by singing that song. Brothers can be a real pain in the butt sometimes!

The "smoke click" part was in reference to the smoking incident; the "thistle foot" part was because when I would go barefoot and step on a thistle it would hurt, and I would cry. It was the "boy and girl" part that really "got my goat!"

When I was eight, I went to New York City with my ma to see the Barnum and Bailey Circus, and I saw Roy Rogers

4: MORE CHILDHOOD MEMORIES

and Dale Evans. It was an exciting experience for me as I loved Roy and his horse, Trigger!

This was the first time I had ever been in the "Big City!" And I had never seen a black man before. We were in a taxi at night, and it was very dark, and so was he. He turned around and gave me such a beautiful smile and his teeth were so white against his dark skin. I asked my ma, "Why are his teeth so white?" He laughed and really smiled then. I never asked why he was black, just asked why he had such white teeth. I was color blind then, and I still am.

We visited my grandparents when we were in the city. I felt like such a big girl because they allowed me to walk around the block with the postman as he delivered the mail. That was the highlight of each day for me as I helped him.

Another fun childhood memory back on the farm is when I would take a bath in our old claw foot bathtub. My ma used to shampoo my hair, and she would spike it up and make all sorts of funny hairdos. It was great fun. I always took a bath on Saturday night so I would be ready for Church on Sunday morning.

In ninth grade I won GRAND PRIZE in the school fair for making an American Flag out of bachelor button flowers. They were red, white, and blue flowers. Of course, this was my ma's idea as she was very creative. We always had an area in the garden for our flowers. I love flowers to this day, and my ma used to always have a bouquet on the kitchen table, which is a tradition I now carry on.

As I got older, I helped with the haying, which always made me sneeze as I have allergies and hay fever. Originally, my pa and brothers put the loose hay in the hay-mow with a huge hayfork. After that we got a round baler, and then after my grandpa came to live with us, he bought us a square baler.

After my brothers went away to college, I used to drive the tractor, but I didn't have to lift any hay bales. Now, this reminds me of my S.O.B.—Tim. (As in ... S̲ort O̲f B̲rother ... not what you were thinking, I bet!)

He came to live with us when he was thirteen. He helped with the haying for the summer. But then eventually he came to live with us full time. So, he was like a third brother. I remember one day he was lifting hay bales onto a wagon, and I was driving the tractor. He was so slow I wanted to scream!

He later entered the Air Force, and after he was honorably discharged, he went to nursing school and became an RN, like my ma and me. We now live twenty minutes away from each other and talk to each other on the phone often. Even though we disagree on lots of issues, political and religious, we still can laugh and forgive each other for our different views. It is good to be able to talk about anything and still get along without any anger. I wish more people in this world could do the same. We have fun sharing childhood memories of growing up on the farm. He loved my ma and always told me that she was his best friend.

4: MORE CHILDHOOD MEMORIES

Be sure to enjoy the little things in life—horses, flowers, people—and remember things don't always go the way we want them to. But HANG IN THERE and enjoy the ride. And don't kick off any emergency brakes at drive-in- theaters! And always remember to let your creativity shine!

5
AUNTIE FRANCIES

As a kid I would ask Auntie FranCies, "How old are you?"

Her reply was always the same, "Old enough to mind my own business!"

She drank pickle juice and ate unpeeled oranges. She surrounded herself with cats, lots and lots of cats. When she passed to eternal life, my brothers went into her room and counted her cats, twenty-nine was the total. They were indoor/outdoor cats. More cat stories to follow.

Auntie FranCies' name was Celestine E. FranCies, and she was a drama, math, and art teacher in NYC before she had to retire at a young age. She had a goiter and had surgery for it and never returned to work. But she sure worked hard at her second job of having a summer business on the lake.

One of my favorite memories of Auntie FranCies is when she coached my oldest brother, Bill, for his prize-speaking contest. My ma and I used to be on the other side of her door, in the living room, where we would laugh and laugh

5: AUNTIE FRANCIES

as she made him repeat it over and over until he got it right.

She also helped me when I took prize speaking and recited by memory an article called "Someday Maria" by Eddie Albert, in *Guideposts Magazine* in January of 1962. (The actual story is in "Guidepost Classics: Eddie Albert on Letting God Lead.") I won the contest at our local school and went to Regionals that year, so she was a good teacher. Be sure to look it up and read the article that had a profound effect on my life when I was an adult. More about that later. Don't miss it as the best is yet to come!

After I had grown up and moved to Florida, Auntie FranCies would come down to visit us. Many of the neighborhood kids would come to our home and sit by her feet and listen to her recite poetry by memory. One time she sat outside, and she made a recording for us. Our basset hound, Clyde, came up to her as she recited poetry and put his chin right up in her lap. Dogs are a good test of character. She was an amazing lady and a wonderful surrogate grandma for me.

Another fond memory of her was when she had her hired man plant flowers around the farmhouse. My brother and his family had been visiting and were getting ready to return home. They stood nearby waiting to say goodbye. The hired man said, "Miss FranCies, Don is ready to go."

After he repeated this several more times, she replied, "Yes and you're planting marigolds!" as she poked at the ground with her cane to show him where to plant the next marigold.

She used to sift the dirt before planting her flowers. Pansies were one of her favorite flowers, and she always planted them along the side of the farmhouse. To this day they are my favorite flower, and Johnny jump-ups too.

When I was young, I used to enjoy being next to her to "help" her in the mess hall down at the lake while she cooked for her boarders. I remember cutting up lard for her pies. And I loved setting the table for them. Whenever I helped her with anything, she would give me caramel candies as a treat. My poor brothers would work hard doing things for her, but for their treat, she would only give them a banana!

My first experience with the Catholic Church was at the age of eight when I listened to Archbishop Fulton Sheen on the radio with "Auntie FranCies." She was a Catholic, but she never pushed her faith on anyone. I was raised a Baptist. More about that later . . . be patient!

In the fall she had several NYC detectives come up to go hunting. They were great fun, and one of them used to bring clothes up from the city for me. Another one let me shoot his rifle; now that was a "real kick!"

When Auntie FranCies was down at the lake working, my brothers would take great delight when the oldsters, "Uncle Ed" and "Uncle James," sat in their rocking chairs on the front porch of our farmhouse. They would go into her room and toss our dog, Louie, into the mix of cats. Those kitties would go flying out of the wooden contraption she had made allowing them to go in and out through the window. What a racket those kitties would make as

5: AUNTIE FRANCIES

they all scrambled to fit out of the window at the same time. The old fellows would almost have heart attacks with all the commotion! It was great fun for my brothers!

We grew up on a farm on a beautiful lake in the foothills of the Catskill Mountains. We lived a simple and meager life: summers were spent with my brothers helping with the haying, and I loved playing with the city kids. I remember playing with a city girl my age. We pretended we cooked breakfast, as we were "baking" on a rock down by the lake.

One day a city boy wanted to ride my horse, Traveller. I told him this might not be a good idea, but he would not listen. The teenager got on my horse's back, and my horse took off like a shot out of a gun. As Traveller ran across our meadow, I yelled to the boy, "When you get to the barn, be sure to duck, or he will take your head off!" My horse always headed for the barn if anyone he did not know got onto his back.

So what is the lesson from this chapter? Never ask an old lady how old she is, and don't jump on a horse if you don't know how to ride!

6

MY LOVE FOR THE "TOP LOT" AND FOR GOD BEGINS

At the age of eight I progressed up the hill to a stone wall just off the edge of the "Top Lot." Many times, I would sit by that stone wall under the trees and take delight no one knew where I was. Little did I know then God always knew where I was! And He always watched over "Little Lesley." It was a slice of Heaven, and it was here I began having thoughts of God and felt His presence.

Every field on a farm has a name. The "Top Lot" was named that because it is the highest elevation on the farm, at 2,150 feet above sea level. I liked to sit on the stone wall at the edge of the Top Lot, and I used to talk to God and feel close to Him up there on my "little piece of solitude and silence." I felt only God knew where I was, and He always listened. My love for the Top Lot began, and many years later it played a significant part in my adult

6: MY LOVE FOR THE "TOP LOT"

life. One day, many, many, years later, GOD would give me a "GRAND PLAN" to accomplish up on HIS Top Lot and my future "mission" in life. For now, I shall keep you in suspense.

I was almost hit by a car when I was around the age of eight. I ran out from the farmhouse toward the barn. A car came up from the lake between two buildings, one the woodshed and the other the shop. It was another "close call" for me. And once again, God looked out for me as I was not hit by that car. God had greater plans for me in the future. And God has plans for YOU too! To God be all the Glory!

Another memory of me as a child was when we used to have a large, round, high tank holding gasoline. Now this experience is only known by me as I am sure if I had shared it with anyone, they would not have believed me. But I remember rising in the air and "flying" a few feet. It was a peaceful flight, and I returned to the ground very gently. I had trouble believing it myself, and I still do have trouble believing it. It only happened one time, and just for about eight seconds. I am sure if I had shared this story with anyone, they would have said that I was "sniffing the gas," and maybe you will say that too! This is the first time I have ever shared this story with anyone! Do you wonder why? And I <u>wasn't</u> sniffing the gas!

One day I walked with another kid on a dirt road a few hills over from ours. We saw a black bear in the woods down the hill from us. When I told my brothers they did not believe me and still tease me about it to this day. I can still see that black bear in my mind's eye! So maybe that will help you understand why I did not share the above story about my flight with anyone.

I attended the First Baptist Church with my family. It was difficult to go every Sunday, especially in the winter and doing chores before Church. But I remember one time my pa was out in the car waiting for my ma and me to get in the car. My ma was in the bathroom putting on her lipstick. My pa was blowing the horn as loud and as frequently as he could to try to hurry her along. Well, I was watching her apply her lipstick, and I could see that she was going very slowly. The horn kept blowing, and I could see she had an impish smile on her face. She was showing him! To me that was hilarious.... All I could think was "GO, MOMMA!" Guess she showed him who was boss!

When we were able to attend the Baptist Church, I remember the minister preaching about how we were all sinners. I used to think, "I'm not a sinner, what is he talking about?" I thought this as I lusted over all the good-looking guys in the choir! Sinner? *Who, me?* Not me! Of course, we are all sinners and fall short of the glory of God! (Romans 3:23)

Have you ever had any moments you have not shared with others out of fear they would not believe you? Any black bear stories?

7
AND NOW A LITTLE MORE ABOUT OUR "PA"

Our Father (a.k.a. Pa) was a very intelligent man even though he never attended college. He was an avid reader and was self-educated. He was a "jack of all trades;" he was a school bus driver because no one would come up to our mountain to pick up the local kids for school. He was also a farmer, a substitute teacher, the President of the School Board, a janitor, and he knew how to work on the boilers. He also represented the kitchen workers and bus drivers. He would go into the principal's office if there were any issues with his coworkers needing to be resolved. He was also the local tax assessor at one time. So he wore many hats. One year, a friend ran for an elected position, and Pa went all over the hills spreading the word about how this man was well qualified. His friend won the election because country folk for miles around showed up to vote, thanks to our "Pa!"

He raised me to believe in myself; I could do anything I set my mind to. And this surely came in handy for my future because I would definitely need the gift of PERSEVERANCE. He always encouraged me to do well in school and in life.

He was "rough and gruff," but I always knew he loved me even though he was not demonstrative. He always encouraged me to be and do my best and always helped me with any problems I may have encountered or questions I had growing up.

If any of us misbehaved, Pa would say, "Ma get the strap." The strap was a leather strap used to sharpen the razor blades in a barbershop. One day we had been playing in the school bus and that was a BIG "NO, NO!" So I heard those words and almost froze. He put me over his knees and hit me one time, very gently. I was no dummy, so I screamed bloody murder! And he quickly stopped. That was the one and only time he used the strap on me. My brothers might tell a different story. We all usually behaved whenever he raised his voice. That was all we needed to straighten up. Do you think we need more "pa's" like this today?

One day my pa was going to feed the kitties out in the barn. He climbed the ladder to reach the haymow. He was carrying a saucer of nice warm milk up to the kitties up above. One kitty was so excited she fell over the edge of the entrance to the haymow. As she fell down, her claw went through my father's nose. He did not spill one drop of milk as he retreated down the steps of the ladder with the kitty still hanging onto his nose. OUCH!

My pa always encouraged me to read. I read quite a lot, but I was not fond of this idea. However, again, I

7: AND NOW A LITTLE MORE ABOUT OUR "PA"

persevered and read many different books. When I was thirteen, I read a book by John J. Gunter titled *DEATH BE NOT PROUD*. It was the story of his son, Johnny, suffering from a brain tumor and finally dying from it. Years later, after I had graduated as an RN, my first job was at the Neurological Institute in NYC. Amazingly, that is where Johnny had been treated for his brain cancer many years earlier.

Some of my poppa's expressions used to make me laugh. Here are a few of his country quotes. Instead of just saying "see you later," he would say "see you later, God willing and if the creek don't rise." And "You can't make a silk purse out of a sow's ear." And when it was very cold, "It's colder than a witch's tit!" "An empty can makes the most noise." And one that is timeless, "This country/world is going to Hell in a hand basket!" Ponder that thought for a moment; I wonder what he'd be thinking of the country/world today?

Do any of these expressions make sense to you? Hope so!

It is so important to read to your little ones. Encourage them to read by themselves as they get older because you never know what book might change their lives. Give them the gift of good books and encourage them to read as little ones and as teens.

And always remember to "hang in there" like the little kitty!

8
OUCH! AND SOME HAPPY MEMORIES TOO

In third grade I broke my right arm at school. My friend and I skipped on the terrazzo floor. She accidently tripped me, and down I went.... *BAM*! OUCH! I had a compound fracture of my right arm, which means the bone poked through the skin. I had to ride in the back seat of a car all the way to the closest hospital, which was about thirty minutes away. My arm was on a pillow, and the school nurse sat in the front seat as I sat in the back seat alone as one of the janitors drove the car. Every bump was very painful. It was the worst break in the history of the hospital up until that time. Of course, I fell in love with my X-Ray tech., Ralph. I was boy crazy even at the age of eight!

They set my arm in the emergency room by first "knocking me out" with ether. So it was not a pleasant experience for me, as ether causes much throwing up. My ma was a registered nurse, and she was able to work in the pediatric ward that night so she could keep an eye on me. During

8: OUCH! AND SOME HAPPY MEMORIES TOO

the night I had quite a laugh as my ma was changing the diaper of a baby boy who had just had hernia surgery that day; suddenly I saw a stream of urine flying high in the sky. Somehow that made me laugh, and I was able to forget the pain of my broken arm.

Over the next two years I broke my right arm two more times. YES, I was a little "tomboy!" The second time I broke my arm, I was out of the cast from the first break for about a month. I was down at the lake and running up a hill, and the rocks came out from under my feet and down I went. OUCH, break number two! I remember Momma making me take off my dirty T-shirt before I went to the emergency room.

Break number three was when I was in our kitchen playing with a ping pong paddle. My oldest brother sat in the rocking chair, and he said, "Give it to me!" Well, remember my independent nature? I did not want to give it to him. After a few more times of him telling me I needed to give it to him, I threw it at him, gently of course! NOT! Then he got up and grabbed my left arm and swung me around a few times and let go. *BAM*, down I went onto the hard floor, which was break number three, right arm, but at least this time it was in a different place on my right arm, it was on my upper arm. I was not able to have a cast the third time, and I had to take my arm out of the sling three times a day and rotate it around so my shoulder would not "freeze up."

Today my parents would have been investigated for child abuse. But this was far from the truth... unless making me change my dirty T shirt would be considered child abuse?!

Perhaps these times in the emergency room may have led to me wanting to be a RN in the emergency department many years later?

At the age of thirteen my parents decided I needed to learn how to "slow dance." So they assigned my oldest brother, Bill, to do the job. I was a major klutz. And he kept yelling at me "DO NOT LEAD!" I also used to step on his toes. I never did learn how to dance as I still lead, in dancing and in many other areas of my life. Being a leader became a common thread in my adult life; more about that later.

At the age of thirteen my best friend was a handsome horse named Traveller; he was a birthday gift from my paternal grandfather. I loved to travel with Traveller. And travel I did, riding him all over the farm and down into the valley. He was named after Confederate General E. Lee's horse. He was the most famous horse during the American Civil War. My brother, Don, insisted we name our dog ABE, after President Abe Lincoln. So, we had a Southern horse and a Northern dog. He was a great dog too!

My horse feared snakes in the road and a house that had a zigzag different-colored roof. And he would not walk over a wooden covered bridge. I had to dismount and drag him across. He would always "slam on his breaks" at each of these things, and I would almost go flying over his head. Again, God was looking out for me.

Living on a farm, we always had lots of dogs over the years: Louie, Abe, May, Flicka, Diaga, and Tillie, just to name a few. We also had lots of cats, cows, calves,

8: OUCH! AND SOME HAPPY MEMORIES TOO

chickens, pigs, and a goat. I remember stories of both of my brothers riding pigs at a neighbor's farm.

I loved one of Auntie FranCies' cats; it was a grey kitty. And one time I listened to a radio program about what it meant to be well groomed. They spoke of cutting your hair, shaving if you were a guy and being clean among other things. Well, after I heard this, I decided I should "groom" the little gray kitty. And so I trimmed her whiskers very short. Well, Auntie FranCies found the poor little kitty lost out in the tall grass. She could not go forward. Evidently, unbeknownst to me, cats use their whiskers to navigate; the whiskers help them know if they can fit through a space or not. Who knew? Not me!

We had chickens too and a mean old rooster, but he didn't last long as he attacked one of my brothers and my father put a quick end to him!

There were always wild animals and birds around too: turkeys, geese, hummingbirds, all types of wild birds, blue heron, ducks, coyotes, porcupines, groundhogs, black bear, deer, bobcats, and eagles, to name a few. Once again God looked out for me.

Are you a leader or a follower? Be sure to follow the right One! And lead others to Him. To God be all the Glory!

9

THE FUN AND THE SAD TIMES OF LIFE ON THE FARM

Milking the cows was always an experience, some good, some bad. One fun experience was when my brother Don and I would do the chores together whenever he would come home from college. We had a few kitties in the barn, to keep the mouse population down, and my brother and I would love to squirt the cow's milk directly from the cow into the mouth of the kitties always standing by waiting for their breakfast of fresh cow's milk.

A few unpleasant experiences of being a farm girl was having to shovel the cow manure into the "Honey wagon." And in the springtime the cows would eat the fresh green grass. Well, you might be able to imagine what that did to the cows' digestive systems. It was always a joy to have a sloppy wet poop covered tail swat you in the face while doing the milking. I know... GROSS! And of course, some cows liked to kick when you milked them.

9: THE FUN AND THE SAD TIMES OF LIFE

One of my concerns as a young teenage girl was that I did not want to smell like a cow as I had to go to school in the mornings after doing the chores. So when I came in from the barn, I would wash my hair and stand on a chair in front of the hot air vent to dry my hair. We did not have a hair dryer at the time. Being a farm girl had its good and not-so-good times.

For my thirteenth birthday, Grandpa gave me the love of my life, up until that time. He was a handsome horse, and I named him Traveller. I mentioned him earlier in this story, and I loved him so much. We had many awesome adventures together. My horse was very protective, and one day a boy and I walked along the "wood road." This is a wide path circling part of the "Top Lot." My horse came up behind him and put his nose in the boy's back and shoved him about three feet. He was a very jealous horse, and I loved him too. My horse did not know this guy was gay, and at the time neither did I. I didn't even know what it meant.

I found that out one day during band practice. Another member of the band handed me a letter one day, and it was a letter from the gay guy to him, and it was a love letter. I was very confused and innocent. The guy who showed me the letter was <u>not</u> gay, and he knew I liked the other guy. So he wanted me to know the circumstances right away as, of course, being very "boy crazy," I was enamored with both guys. So as I got onto the bus that day, I showed the letter to my pa; remember he was our school bus driver. He then explained such things about life to me. Wow, who knew? Not me!

The gay guy and I became best friends, and I listened to his pain all throughout high school. Remember this was back in the '60s when this type of thing was always kept a secret. We would write letters to each other over the summer, and his pain was so intense and so sad. We would also get together over the summer, and I would listen to his heart ache. He trusted me, and I always kept his secret. As an adult, he did finally "come out of the closet." So that is the reason I can share his story now. He has since passed to eternal life. May he rest in peace.

I learned compassion through our friendship. My father was glad I liked him, and he let me go to school dances with him because he knew I was "safe" with him. Our friendship kept him going through his high school years, as he did not share his secret with anyone else. Once again this gave me compassion for others' heartaches. Enough about "real life issues!"

And now more about Traveller. At the age of fourteen I would arise at 5 a.m. to help my father with the chores of milking the cows. My two brothers were away from home by then, and I was left to help my pa on the farm. Off into the deep woods I would go, with my faithful companion, my dog Abe. Sometimes the trees would cast looooooong shadows as I searched for the cows early in the morning. My horse was originally from Colorado. He was a Western horse who loved to "round up the cows!" He used to sleep with them, and sometimes I think he thought he was a cow himself! I used to call the cows to come to me by yelling "COOOOOO BOSSSSSSS!" And as soon as my horse heard

9: THE FUN AND THE SAD TIMES OF LIFE

me calling the cows, he would round them up for me. The neighbors a half a mile away could hear me calling them. And others way down in the valley also heard me.

As an adult, once I had converted to the Catholic Church (that's another long story, stay tuned!), the ability to project my voice came in handy as I became a lector and had to make those sitting way in the back of the chapel hear me as I read the readings of the day. We didn't have a microphone at the time.

God taught me to have **NO FEAR** through these childhood experiences. I was not afraid of the dark. Traveller would help me bring our cows to the barn for their morning milking and again late in the afternoon. Each cow knew exactly where their stanchion was in the barn, and every cow had a name. We had a small farm, only twenty-nine cows.

One time, one of our cows delivered a calf out in the woods. My brother Don and I went to search for them. We found them, and he put the calf into the wagon with me, and then he drove the tractor as fast as he could. The "momma" cow wanted to get to her baby and tried to jump into the wagon as I was holding her little one. Once again it taught me to PERSEVERE and to have NO FEAR! Even though at the time I was scared to death! Once again God was looking out for me!

Another time we had a calf that had paralyzed back legs. I asked my ma if I could give her liquid Jell-o, then I enlisted my brother, Don, to help me by putting a stick under her back legs to try to hold her up as I had her drink the liquid Jell-o. Of course, nothing helped, so I had to accept the fact it was hopeless. Again, it gave me compassion for animals too.

One of my jobs was watering the calves in a fenced area. I filled a big tub with water, and they all came running over and drank the water within minutes. So, I went into the house and got more water for them. Again, they drank all the water within a few minutes. I knew something must be wrong, so I ran and got my pa. He called the vet, and he discovered the calves had been able to reach across the fence and eat a plant called purple nightshade. This is very deadly plant, and all those beautiful calves died. That was a sad day for me. But I think that incident also influenced me to have even more compassion for animals and people.

Another very sad experience as a farm girl was one morning when I discovered that one of our calves had died overnight. We used to keep our calves in a pen in the barn. She was tied to the wall with a rope. She evidently tried to jump over the door lying sidewise across the opening to the pen. She accidentally hung herself. That was a shocking and sad experience for me. The life of a farm girl is one of sadness and joy. At one time I thought of becoming a vet, but I knew I would not be able to handle huge animals by myself.

And now for a happy memory. A fun thing to do with the calves was when they were being weaned from their momma cows. I learned how to teach the calves to drink milk from a bucket. I had to put my fingers in their mouths so they would start to suck on my fingers. Then I would gently lower their head down into the bucket until they

9: THE FUN AND THE SAD TIMES OF LIFE

reached the milk. They soon learned how to drink the milk from the bucket.

Hope this chapter wasn't too graphic for you all. Just wanted to share that farm kids go through the good and the bad, and we survive!

No matter what you are going through, praying you will survive too. God has plans for you!

10

MY WONDERFUL MA
"THIS TOO SHALL PASS."

My ma grew up in Halifax, Nova Scotia. Her childhood was riddled with very difficult experiences. She was six years old when she was walking to school on the morning of Dec. 6, 1917. The Halifax Explosion occurred, and it was the largest "manmade" explosion prior to the WWII atom bomb. Buildings and houses were built sloping down hills along the river. This meant the concussion from the explosion was enormous.

A French cargo ship *SS Mont-Blanc* had collided with the Norwegian vessel *SS Imo* in the waters of Halifax, Nova Scotia, Canada. The *Mont-Blanc* was laden with high explosives (war munitions) and caught fire and exploded. At least 1,782 people died, and 9,000 others were injured after the blast. The anchor of one of the ships was found on land over a quarter mile from the detonation site.

Some children looked out the windows when the explosion happened, and when the glass shattered, they were blinded.

10: MY WONDERFUL MA

A school for the blind was later started to help these little ones. It was the largest mass blinding in Canadian history, and it birthed the Canadian National Institute for the Blind.

My mother's house was partly demolished and the stairway to the upstairs hung on the side of the house. She ran home and we were told that because she was the littlest and the lightest one, she was the one chosen to climb up the stairway to retrieve the family valuables located upstairs in the house.

She had a difficult life as a child as her mother died when she was thirteen. Her mother used to work in a factory where they painted luminescent/radioactive paint on the face of watches. This allowed the watches to light up in the dark. The ladies doing the painting would use their tongues to make the tip of the paintbrush thin and pointed so they could paint the numbers on the watches. She got radiation poisoning and died, as did many others. These girls were called the "Radium Girls."

Her father was an engineer on a locomotive on a railroad in Canada, so it was probably very difficult for him to work and raise his children. So sometime after this my ma immigrated to the USA from Canada as someone in NYC sponsored her.

As an adult she attended nursing school at Vassar Brothers Hospital School of Nursing and graduated in 1933. She was a very kind, loving person and always helped others. She was a registered nurse, and the neighbors would call her all hours of the day and night to ask her medical questions. I remember as a child being afraid when she gave others advice on the phone, I used to worry "what if she tells them the wrong thing and someone dies?" No one ever did, and she was always available to help anyone at any time. Everyone loved my mother.

We had a "party line" on the phone, and she and her best friend, a close neighbor, used to talk on the phone for hours and of course occasionally "listen in" to the neighbors' conversations.

She had a great sense of humor and was also very creative. I thank God I received a bit of her good humor and creativity.

I remember listening to Tennessee Ernie Ford on the radio with her. This gave me a love for Country Gospel. And I still love his songs and other Country Gospel music singers. I give thanks to my momma for introducing me to praise and worship music.

She always thought of others, and during the winter she would heat up a soapstone and cover it in flannel and bring it up to my bedroom at nighttime to keep my feet warm. She was a loving momma! God rest her soul.

When my mom was a student nurse at Vassar Brothers Hospital, she and another nurse took care of a patient in an iron lung. The story is in *Time Magazine* on May 1, 1950; the article is "Medicine; In an Iron Lung," and it was a tragic story of how polio can ravage a body. She was very close to Bird Sweet's family for many years, even after he died. My parents used his name as a middle name for their firstborn son.

When in nursing school, she was quite a jokester. One time she hid herself in an operating room sterilizer;

10: MY WONDERFUL MA

obviously it was not running at the time. When her classmates entered the O.R., they would open the door to the sterilizer, and she would jump out and scare them. Another escapade was in the winter when the student nurses slid down the hill behind the hospital on metal bedpans.

Now, back to the farm, Ma used to own a fat little dog named Flicka. And the pooch and my ma had something in common; they both used to be a bit "gassy." If my ma would "let one go," she would look at the dog and yell, "<u>FLICKA!</u>" And blame the dog. I told you she had a great sense of humor!

One day she won a contest from the local radio station, 81 W.G.Y., and as a prize she was able to visit the radio station and receive a reward by Howard Tupper, the local DJ. My two brothers and I were able to be in the studio too. I was probably about three and was so cute with bows in my hair. The microphone was open, and I innocently announced to the whole listening audience, "I have to go to the bathroom!"

Ma's driving experiences were not the best. The "final straw" was when all three of us kids were in the car and she backed up into the shop.... *BAM*! The Shop was a wooden building close to the farmhouse. She never drove again. Poor Momma!

Lesson from this chapter? Do you think we all need a dog named Flicka to blame our flatulence ("tooting") on?

And always try to remember my ma's favorite saying whenever you are going through a tough time, "This too shall pass!"

11

B.M. IN THE A.M. GRANDPA COMES TO LIVE WITH US

I was thirteen when my paternal grandmother passed to eternal life. God rest her soul. Then Grandpa came to the farm from NYC to live with us.

Every morning, he would come downstairs and proceed to tell my ma all about his bowel movement that morning. He would go into full detail about size, color, and consistency. Remember she was a registered nurse, but I wasn't yet! YUCK! Now that was quite an unpleasant experience for a thirteen-year-old!

Every afternoon, as soon as I would return from school, I had to play a card game called Three Handed Bridge with my ma and g'pa. Now that was also so much fun for a thirteen-year-old. NOT!

My grandpa was a very intelligent man. He was the principal of a school in NYC, and he founded a school in a town

11: B.M. IN THE A.M.

in Upstate NY. I found all his accolades and have saved them for our family history.

One of my fun memories about my g'pa was when his first great grandchild was born. She was in a swing hanging from the doorway to the kitchen. He used to sing to her, not with words, but with one word repeatedly. He would sing "bye bye, bye bye, etc., etc." I can still hear him singing it. He really enjoyed the baby, and that made me happy too.

My favorite memory is when g'pa gave me Traveller, my horse, when I was thirteen.

My dear grandpa died of hepatitis from receiving a shot with an unsterilized needle at the local doctor's office. Now if that were today, we would be millionaires!

Any lessons from this chapter? Guess we all must take the good with the bad! " BMs in the a.m." weren't so bad after g'pa gave me my horse!

12

A BAD AND A GOOD YEAR FOR ME

When I was in ninth grade, my ma had a mental breakdown. My pa kept her home instead of having her admitted to the psychiatric hospital. This was a very difficult year for me, as my brothers were already away from home. However, once again this helped me have compassion and persevere and "never give up."

One time she was very combative, and as my pa was trying to restrain her, she ripped the pocket of his pants. He yelled to me to "call the doctor!" The Doc came over and gave her a tranquilizer shot to calm her down. So, my ninth grade was "quite a trip!" This was the only time I had seen her in such a condition, and it lasted off and on my whole ninth grade year until she finally got somewhat back to normal.

That year helped me to get closer to my pa as he had to explain a lot of things about life to me that year. Her illness gave me compassion for those who suffer from

12: B.M. IN THE A.M.

mental illness. And I realized she probably had these issues partly because of her difficult childhood experiences.

One day I made the mistake of asking my ma what a "rubber" was. She went really "off the wall!" I told her the boys were throwing one around in the lunchroom at school. Needless to say, I never asked her any more questions after that experience. My pa became both the pa and the ma figure, and I asked him any questions I had after that. It helped me get closer to my pa as he had to keep the family together and keep on keeping on. I never got angry with my ma because I knew she couldn't help the illness that had taken over her life.

Now for another ninth-grade experience. As I mentioned earlier, I was in prize speaking class, and I had chosen a story by the actor, Eddie Albert, the star of the TV show *Green Acres*. It was in a *Guideposts Magazine* in January of 1962, "Someday Maria." It was about how he adopted a little girl from Spain. His story "planted a seed in my heart" to one day adopt a baby from another country. I always thought I would have a baby first and then adopt the opposite sex. God had other plans. Stay tuned for "the rest of the story" in a future chapter.

13

SNOW AND FREEZING COLD EXPERIENCES AS A TEEN

My pa was our school bus driver because no one else would drive to our mountain to pick us up for school. He drove all over and picked up kids from all the hills around. Pa and I would leave for school at 7:30 a.m., after finishing the morning milking. We would arrive at the school at 9 a.m. I was the first one on the bus in the morning and the last one off in the afternoon. I was fortunate in one way because I was able to sit right next to the heater in the winter. And I also had the "privilege" of taking attendance every day. All to be repeated in reverse and not arriving home until late afternoon. All to begin again with milking and chores, homework, dinner, and getting ready for school the next day. Bedtime was 9 p.m.; wake up time was 5 a.m. to milk the cows again.

If the weather was very bad, the principal of the school would call my father, and if my pa said he could not drive

13: SNOW AND FREEZING COLD EXPERIENCES

due to the snowdrifts, then the principal would cancel school. One morning he called, and my ma answered the phone. He asked, "Is Bill there?" At the time she still had a very strong Scottish accent and she replied, "He's ooooottt in the beeeern." Translated meant, "He's out in the barn!" That still gives us all a laugh even to this day!

Oftentimes my brothers would have to put the chains on the school bus in the winter. And sometimes they had to shovel in front of the snowplow to help the plow get through the deep snow. In the springtime the road would be washed out where a pond overflowed over the road. My brothers would have to throw rocks in the road so the bus could pass.

One winter, after my brothers were already away from home, my father drove the school bus in a snowstorm. I was sixteen, and we had gotten stuck in the snow not far from home, near the outlet of the lake. We were the only two on the bus. He decided to walk across the frozen lake, but he wanted me to walk along the road to get home; it was about a mile. That day I had worn a dress to school, so my knees were exposed to the cold. I was trudging through the snow, and I was about a quarter of a mile from home when I realized I could not feel my knees any longer. I looked down, and my knees were swollen with water and my face was numb.

I was afraid I was going to die. However, it also gave me, once again, a "never give up" attitude, and I decided I was <u>NOT</u> going to die out there in the cold and snow. So I kept trudging along until I stumbled into the house.

My ma, being a registered nurse, knew my situation and immediately went into "go mode!" She got a pan of lukewarm water and started pouring it over my knees. I had a case of frostbite for sure. My face was so cold all I could do was mumble. This experience, once again, taught me to persevere and to "never give up!" The best part about that incident was I was able to miss gym class for three weeks. YAY! I hated gym class because I was still such a klutz! Once again, God was looking out for me.

Another snow event happened when I was sixteen. My pa and I were on the way out to the barn to do the chores. The snow was very deep, up to my waist, and he was leading the way and making a pathway for me. I was carrying two pails of hot water from the house out to the barn; halfway there I looked up to Heaven and I mumbled, "GET ME OUT OF HERE!" By the time we arrived at the barn, which was about 150 feet away, I realized the hot pails of water were now cold pails of water.

I must have been complaining a bit because my pa said, "What's the matter?"

I grumbled, "I'm COLD."

He replied, "Take a deep breath and you will be fine."

I said, "IF I TAKE A DEEP BREATH, MY LUNGS WILL FREEZE!"

Later, when we turned on the radio, we heard that it was 50 degrees BELOW ZERO with the wind chill factor! I milked eight cows by hand and their teats were very cold that day. Once again, this experience gave me a "never

13: SNOW AND FREEZING COLD EXPERIENCES

give up attitude!" Of course, it took me several more years before I finally got out of the cold weather. Now, that is a whole 'nother story I will share later!

Keeping you in suspense once again!

14

EXCHANGE STUDENT EXPERIENCES

At the age of seventeen, during the summer between junior and senior year of high school, I was chosen to be an exchange student to Lima, Peru. It was the first year our small school was in this program. Two other students from my class were chosen also: one went to Lima and one of my best friends went to Colombia.

This was an experience that changed my life and also gave me compassion for the poor. When I was in Lima, my Peruvian father drove his wife and me to their hacienda (large farm). He seemed very nervous as he drove through the mountains. I did not know why until much later. There were guerrillas in the high mountains of Peru, and they liked to kidnap Americans for ransom. Who knew? Not an innocent seventeen-year-old girl, me!

When I was on the hacienda, I met the Inca Indians who helped run my Peruvian father's farm. They were beautiful Native Indians of Peru; they were very kind and loving.

14: EXCHANGE STUDENT EXPERIENCES

They made a Pachamanca, this is a Quechua word, pacha meaning "earth" and "manca" pot. This consisted of burying a pig in the ground and roasting it over hot coals. I had never experienced this before. It was an educational and emotional experience and taught me to love and to have compassion for the very poor Native Indians of Peru.

My Peruvian "parents" brought a young teenage girl and her baby from the hacienda back to Lima with us. When we approached Lima, it was nighttime, and the city was gleaming with lights from one side of the horizon to the other. This poor girl started crying because, in her sheltered life on the hacienda, she had never seen anything like this before. She was terrified and thought we were being invaded by someone from outer space. It took a while to get her calmed down again. She became the maid for the family. She lived in a small room on top of their house in Lima. This also gave me even more love and compassion for the poor.

While in Lima I went to school with my Peruvian sister. It was my first experience with the Catholic faith, other than listening to Archbishop Fulton Sheen on the radio when I was eight. I did not have a mantilla, so they put a tissue on my head with bobby pins to hold it on. It was all new to me.

I had a very difficult time understanding the English teacher at my Peruvian sister's school. I did not want the other kids to know I could not understand her. After three days I finally found out why I was having so much trouble understanding her English. She had been taught English by a teacher from Georgia, in the USA, and she had a Southern accent in addition to a Spanish accent. That is why I was having such a difficult time understanding her.

I did not speak any Spanish when I arrived in Lima. I only knew enough Spanish to count to ten and ask "where's the bathroom?" So when I was in school, I took my book of Spanish verbs which I studied every day. This came in handy many years later as I helped Spanish-speaking priests and seminarians learn to speak English when they came to our Church.

Another experience I had while in Lima was quite funny, although not while it was occurring, but after I had finally found out what was happening. One morning I looked out of my two-story bedroom window. Lo and behold the street was full of HUGE military tanks, trucks, and Army guys with rifles all marching in unison. I was scared to death as I thought the country was under siege, a coup for sure, they must have been taking over the government! These were my innocent seventeen-year-old thoughts. I was sure I was never going to get to go home to the USA again. Fortunately, a very nice lady friend of the family came and explained to me it was their Independence Day parade. Who knew? Not me!

I made many friends while I was in Lima, Peru and it was a wonderful experience for a little farm girl from the "boonies" of New York. Exchange programs are a wonderful way for young people to learn about other countries and cultures. The next year in high school we had a boy from Bogota, Colombia stay in our home on the farm. He

14: EXCHANGE STUDENT EXPERIENCES

played a very important and amazing role in my future adult life. More about him in another chapter. Keeping you in suspense once again!

My "welcome home from Peru gift" was a milking machine! Pa had bought another milking machine while I was out of the country. That was quite a nice surprise for me because I had always milked eight cows by hand, while he milked twenty with his milking machine. So I guess he missed me a lot while I was gone.

Many years later, after I had moved to Florida, I became a coordinator for the International Exchange Program. I found homes for twenty-five exchange students from Brazil. I also had to plan excursions with all of them. They were great fun and sure loved to party!

Being a farm girl had its good and its bad times, as most people have in life. How about your childhood? Try to focus on the good times, even when it was difficult. I hope the good always outweighs the bad for you.

15
GRADUATION FROM HIGH SCHOOL AND MY NURSING SCHOOL EXPERIENCES

At my high school graduation in 1966, I was quite surprised when the class valedictorian shared my quote with everyone. I had "received" it one night in the middle of the night. It was "Generation after generation, the destiny of this great Nation is now in our hands!" I didn't grasp the meaning of it until years later. It is certainly something to ponder upon in this day and age. Perhaps it is finally coming to fruition? Think about it and ponder it yourself.

Television shows growing up probably influenced me to want to be a registered nurse. I grew up on shows like *Dr. Kildare* (NBC TV medical drama from 1961 to '66), *Ben Casey Neurosurgeon* (medical drama series on ABC from 1961 to 1966) and *Marcus Welby, M.D.* (medical drama TV series on ABC from 1969 to 1976). I learned that many

15: GRADUATION FROM HIGH SCHOOL

people would write to the show's producers asking for medical advice.

Now, time for something hilarious, before I left for nursing school, my father had to take me to the county seat to get some legal paperwork. As he drove, my ma was in the front seat and my brother in the back seat with me. Suddenly, we looked up, and on a very high grassy hill above the road, I saw a "honey wagon" (A.K.A. a wagon full of cow manure) flying down the hill. My brother and I yelled! And of course, that made my pa slow down. My brother then yelled, "Step on the gas!" and the manure spreader flew down the hill and just missed us as it went flying behind our car. It was a very close call, and later all I could think of was the newspaper headlines if it had hit us, "College-bound student killed by a manure spreader!" Once again, God was looking out for me!

After graduation from high school, I followed in Ma's footsteps and was accepted into the same nursing school she had graduated from thirty-three years before me. It was Vassar Brothers Hospital School of Nursing in Poughkeepsie, New York. I took my college classes at Dutchess Community College and did my psychiatric training at Hudson River State Mental Hospital.

I still remember my very first patient as a brand-new student nurse. He was an elderly gentleman, and as I entered his room I said, "Good morning, Mr. W.; how are you?"

His reply was, "MISERABLE!"

Can you imagine being eighteen years old and hearing that as a "wet behind the ears" student nurse?! He was miserable because he was scheduled to be transferred to the State Mental Health Hospital that morning. They had neglected to tell me that in our morning nurses report!

The first evening I worked as a student nurse in the emergency room on February 10, 1968, a newspaper headline article read, "Plane Crash Takes 3 Lives."

The patient I was assigned to had third degree burns from his head to his toes, all except for one small area that was first degree. Third degree burns do not cause pain because the burn is so deep it goes below the pain receptors on the skin. However, first and second-degree burns are painful. So, he was in pain as he had one small area on his body that was not third degree. Of course, he was also in shock, which caused him to be very thirsty. He was awake and alert. I asked one of the registered nurses working on his case if I could give him some water to wet his mouth?

She replied, "Sure!"

Then I asked her, "Should it be sterile water?"

Now this was an innocent question. She knew he would not live for very long because when someone has third degree burns over 99 percent of their body, it is a miracle to be alive at all. But she did not laugh at my dumb question. I stayed up by his head and kept talking to him, and he told me he had been engaged for a year and was supposed to be married in a few months. He asked me to call his fiancé. He gave me her phone number, and of course one of the RNs or a doctor called her with the sad news.

15: GRADUATION FROM HIGH SCHOOL

He was transferred to the Intensive Care Unit. This was my first experience in the ER, and that very night I was going to receive my nurses' cap. It was a very emotional night for me.

I believe that experience once again led to me working in the emergency department in Florida many years later. I worked there for twenty years ... more about that later!

I had an experience with my first Catholic guy while I was in nursing school. One night several of us girls decided to go to a "mixer" dance at a nearby Catholic College. Of course, I fell in love, my first real love, with a Catholic guy. And we had a good, healthy, loving relationship during the years I was studying to become a nurse. When we had a date, I always remember standing at the second-floor kitchen window and waiting for "my guy" to drive up. He was a very talented guy and he played the accordion in a band, and he also played the piano. Many times, he played and sang a song for me, "Scotch and Soda" by the Kingston Trio. He taught me how to play it too. He was a senior at this college, and we went to his Sr. Prom. He missed my nursing school graduation though because he was learning how to fly an airplane, and he had a flying lesson that night, so he was late for my ceremony, and I was not happy about that!

After I graduated from nursing school, I moved to NYC, and he came to visit me. It seems his mother and his grandmother found out I was NOT a Catholic. And they told him, "THAT'S THAT.... DUMP HER!" and so he eventually did. So my first experience with a Catholic boy was not a good one. However, looking back on it now, I am very fortunate he "dumped me" as if we had gotten married, I would have been stuck in Upstate NY freezing my buns off instead of sunning my buns in Sunny South Florida. God was looking out for me again! God is good all the time; all the time God is good.

    Wow, what do I say to you about this chapter? Have you ever been "dumped?" Have you ever had a "honey wagon" try to kill you? Guess we are both fortunate to still be here even through the tough times!

16

COUNTRY GIRLS MOVE TO THE BIG CITY!

After I graduated from nursing school, I started my first job in NYC at Colombia Presbyterian Medical Center at the Neurological Institute.

My nursing school roommate and I lived on the twenty-ninth floor in an apartment at the end of the George Washington Bridge. We walked ten blocks to work every afternoon and back again at 11:30 at night.

The hospital complex had nine hospitals connected by underground tunnels. After my 3-11p.m. shift was over, I walked from the Neurological Institute to where my roommate worked in the Emergency Room. I walked through a very long underground tunnel to meet up with her. I was all alone in one of those tunnels at 11:30 at night. There were all sorts of unnerving noises in the tunnel.

One night when I arrived at the emergency room, I smelled something funny. I asked her, "What is that smell?"

Her reply was, "Oh that is just a patient smoking pot!"

WOW! Remember I was an innocent country girl, but I had to learn fast.

We had to walk ten blocks home to our apartment on the twenty-ninth floor at 11:30 at night. We would run from one bar to the next because there were police phones outside of every bar.

Another nurse friend of ours who had also moved to the "BIG CITY" walked home at three in the afternoon one day. A very BIG guy stood in front of her and said, "I've got a gun," as he showed her his gun in a holster on his chest.

She very calmly replied, "Yep, and it's a nice one too," as she patted the gun and kept walking past him. He stood there in shock!

Living in Uptown Manhattan was a little scary for a twenty-year-old country girl. Riding the subway was quite an experience, and my roommate and I never knew where we were when we walked up the subway stairs to the street. So she would walk all the way to the end of one block, and I would walk all the way to the end of the block in the other direction. When we saw the street signs, we would yell and wave to one another to decide which way to go! Too bad we didn't have cell phones with GPS maps back in the day!

I worked on a private floor, meaning one patient to a room, at the Neurological Institute. We participated in a study of the new drug, L-Dopa, for Parkinson patients. We had to chart and keep track of every symptom. It was very interesting because it was also a teaching hospital. We worked with interns and residents. Oftentimes they

16: COUNTRY GIRLS MOVE TO THE BIG CITY!

depended on the nurses to give them advice. Pretty funny as I was a brand-new RN, but I learned a lot very quickly.

One of my memorable patients was a young guy who had been shot in the back and was paralyzed from the waist down. He had a metal bar over his bed with a contraption attached so he was able to pull himself up. I felt sorry for him because he had no visitors and was very much alone. So to cheer him up I bought a mobile consisting of a mother hen and her baby chicks which I hung on his contraption above him. It brought a smile to his face.

Another guy was in his twenties, and he had a brain tumor. That was my first experience with someone my own age. He reminded me of the book I read when I was a teen, *Death Be Not Proud*. I loved neurological nursing.

Living in the city was fun at times, I recall walking across the George Washington Bridge at 2 a.m. with a Jewish boy, a friend, (this time I was eventually "dumped" because I wasn't Jewish!) from NJ to the Bronx. It was 32 degrees that night and very windy on the bridge. But it sure was lots of fun. I also remember when together we watched the first-time man walk on the moon on July 20, 1969. When Neil Armstrong said the famous words, "That's one small step for man, one giant leap for mankind." Buz Aldrin was the other astronaut.

Once again, God had other plans for me, and one day I won a three-day two-night vacation to Miami, Florida. It was an attempt by a time-share company for me to buy a time share, which I never did; I just went for the vacation. So I flew to Miami with another friend of mine. Before I left on my trip, I applied for a transfer from a private floor to a ward floor. After I returned from Miami, I found out I had received my transfer. Most nurses do not like "ward floors." They had four guys in a room. So that is why I received my transfer so quickly, because most nurses do not like to take care of the "down and outers!" But I loved it.

After I had received my transfer, I returned to the private floor to see who had taken my place. One of the RNs said, "So I hear you just returned from Florida?"

I said, "YES."

And she replied, "My roommate and I are leaving for Florida soon; do you want to come with us?"

Of course, my immediate answer was "YES!"

I did not even care who they were; they could have been mass murderers as far as I knew. But so long as I could get out of the cold weather, I did not care who they were. They were fun girls too. AND THE REST IS HISTORY.

How many wild and crazy things have you done in your life? Stay tuned for more craziness!

17

THREE NURSES IN AN M.G. MIDGET ON A TRIP TO FLORIDA

The owner of the car drove, and one of my other future roommates rotated with me from the front seat to the back seat, which was very cramped as we had luggage too. First stop was in Washington, DC, where we stayed at a YWCA overnight. As I took a shower, someone called out, "Flushing!"

I, being a smart butt, replied "QUEENS!"

Then I found out that when someone is flushing the toilet, the water in the shower turns to HOT scalding water. Who knew? Certainly not this innocent country girl! (FYI, Flushing is a neighborhood in the borourgh of Queens.)

On our trip south, our next stop was Charleston SC, where we met up with Navy guys. My friend in NYC was engaged to one of them, so she arranged for us to meet them. Their submarine was "in port," so we enjoyed having dinner and a movie on a sub. This was followed by a three-day party at one of the married guy's homes. One guy played the base fiddle on a washtub. We had a blast. And of course, one of the nurses traveling with us fell in love with a Navy guy. Once we moved to Ft. Lauderdale, he used to drive from Charleston, South Carolina every weekend. They ended up getting married a few years later. Last I heard, they moved to Michigan and live on a chicken farm, and they had five kids!

Next stop was Fort Lauderdale. We rented a room in a small hotel named with a foreign name meaning "Good Luck!" Well, I guess we should not have been surprised when we opened the door to our room and there were MIRRORS on the ceiling! We dubbed it the "HOOKER HOTEL!" The three of us slept together, just that one night, in a king-sized bed.

The next morning, we flipped open the Yellow Pages and found a hospital nearby. We called and said, "We are three RNs from NYS, and we need jobs!" The director of nursing interviewed all three of us together.

She then said, "Are you able to start working tomorrow night 3-11 shift?"

We said, "NO, we just got here, and we want a vacation first!"

We had our NYS nursing licenses with us, and the director of nursing had probably just made a phone call to our previous employer. Times sure have changed, huh?! So much for background checks!

Then we needed to find a place to live. So we rented a beautiful apartment on the Isle of Venice in Ft. Lauderdale,

17: THREE NURSES IN AN M.G. MIDGET

which was a short walk to the beach. I must confess that sometimes we hitchhiked to the beach too. The apartment was Heavenly. It had a swimming pool, white shag carpeting, and a MAID who came once a week. WOW! And the three of us shared the rent.

Our lives consisted of working the 3 p.m. to 11 p.m. shift, then going out drinking at the bars till they closed at 4 a.m., then we would come home and sleep until 11a.m., then wake up and go to the beach. We would come back to the apartment and take a shower and go to work. This was our daily routine for the first year we were in Ft. Lauderdale. Young and crazy!

We originally had grand plans of becoming the first "traveling nurses." Our original plan was to go to Miami first and work for six months, then move on to New Orleans and travel across the country. Well, those were great plans, but we never even got to Miami. As usual God had other plans!

I worked on the Medical Surgical floor on the 3-11 shift. One of my memorable patients was a poor old guy dying of neck cancer. The other nurses moved him into the utility room. I did NOT like that idea and told them I would NOT allow him to die alone in a utility room. And so I stayed with him and talked with him until he breathed his last. I wanted him to die with dignity, and he did. I hope to meet him in Heaven one day. Pray for me to get there!

Were you young and crazy at one time in your life too?

18

WORKING IN THE EMERGENCY DEPARTMENT

The Present Moment is the ONLY moment we can be sure of.

> "Act as if every day were the last of your life,
> and each action the last you perform."
> —St. Alphonsus Liguori

> "Let us make up for lost time.
> Let us give to God the time that remains to us."
> —St. Alphonsus Liguori

There were two district hospitals, and nurses could transfer from one hospital to another without losing any seniority. So I worked at the second hospital for another year, also on a medical surgical floor. Then I heard there was a new hospital opening that was also a district hospital. District hospitals accepted anyone whether they had money or not.

18: WORKING IN THE EMERGENCY DEPARTMENT

I had always had an interest in working in the emergency department, probably because of my childhood experiences. Remember my first childhood experience with an emergency room? They used to call it emergency room when I was a kid, then about thirty-five years ago the name was changed to emergency department.[1]

After having a few years of medical/surgical experiences under my belt, I decided it was time to try something new. So I called the third district hospital and spoke with the hospital administrator. They did not even have a director of nursing yet, as the hospital was not even open. With my knees knocking, I asked if they had any openings in their emergency department (E.D.)?

"YES" was his immediate answer.

So off I went to the interview where he hired me on the spot to work in the emergency department. Before the hospital opened, we had "on the job" training by the doctors we would be working with. One was a retired surgeon, one was a retired pediatrician, and a few other doctors. Registered nurses on all the shifts worked together to set up the different rooms with supplies and all the equipment we would need. It was a time of "bonding" with one another, and we all became a close-knit team with the doctors and eventually with the paramedics.

Another nurse and I took a "Trauma Nurse Specialist" class in Miami. We were in their emergency department,

---

1. https://smalltownerdoc.com/2017/10/22/whats-in-a-name-er-vs-ed/

and I looked over and saw someone on a stretcher totally covered with a sheet. Of course, I thought they had prepared him to go to the morgue, as I thought the person was dead. As I watched, I noticed the sheet was moving up and down, and I realized they were still breathing and were ALIVE! So I poked the other nurse taking the class with me, and I said, "I think he is alive!"

So we approached the nurses' station, and I spoke with the charge nurse. I told her that the person under the sheet was breathing and ALIVE! I don't know how she kept her composure without laughing at us. She very patiently explained some people from other countries oftentimes cover themselves completely with a sheet when they feel stressed. We were so embarrassed when she told us that was very normal for emergency department patients because that is how they calm themselves. Who knew? Not me! I still laugh about that today, and over the years I worked in the E.D. since then, I experienced it with my own patients many times.

One day I brought home a video tape to watch about trauma. My husband sat next to me as we watched it together. He was an EMT in the fire department when he was in the Air Force. I must admit I had fun watching my husband's reaction to the trauma. He sat in a rocking chair as we watched the video. I looked over at him, and he held onto the arms of the rocking chair and his knuckles were gripped tightly and they were white! I had a good laugh over that.

It must be very difficult for spouses and families of E.D. nurses or ICU nurses because if family members are sick or injured, they must be on death's door before we help them.

18: WORKING IN THE EMERGENCY DEPARTMENT

I remember one time my young son came home from the playground, and he was bleeding from his head. Another boy, his mother was "teacher of the year," had thrown a rock at him. I stopped my poor boy at the front door and made him wait till I went to get a washcloth to stop the bleeding. It wasn't a big emergency to me, poor kid. I hope he has forgiven me by now!

Emergency department nurses must have a good sense of humor to deal with all the stress. Some nurses have PTSD from all the stress of working with patients who are in critical condition. So a good sense of humor helps a lot, and thankfully I do not have PTSD.

I do not mean that we laugh at the patients, but we do laugh at many other things. One time a pipe broke and there was water all over the floor. We got in wheelchairs and rolled ourselves around the E.D.!

It was also great fun to put a patient on a bedpan and then tell them, "When you are finished, push the call bell and ask for the head nurse by name!" She always got even with me at some point. Nurses just gotta have fun!

When the hospital first opened, we also had to prepare the outpatient surgery patients before they went to surgery, and we had to get them ready to go home after surgery. We also had to take care of all the patients receiving blood transfusions and administer IV meds to chemotherapy patients. We used to have to mix the medicines in our E.D. Today all of that is done in the pharmacy department under strict rules to protect those preparing the chemotherapy meds. After a few more years the hospital opened a same day surgery unit and an infusion department, so we were able to take care of emergency patients only.

Some of my memories of working in the E.D. were funny, but many were sad. We used to have an old homeless guy we nicknamed "BUMPY" because he had bumps all over his body. He was an alcoholic, and once a month he would get "rolled," meaning beaten up, and they would steal his Social Security money from him. Whenever he was brought into the E.D. by ambulance, I would always be the one caring for him. He liked me because I treated him with dignity. He would bite, kick, swear, and spit at anyone else that went near him.

We had a nickname for those who came into the E.D. often.... We called them "frequent flyers." Early one morning, on one of the coldest nights in Florida, my dear "Bumpy" was brought in as a DOA (Dead On Arrival), and I was sad, but at the same time I knew he was finally at rest where no one could hurt him any longer. RIP, "Bumpy." He sure suffered a lot down here on Earth, and I hope to see him in Heaven one day! Pray for me to get there!

Another wild and crazy memory was when I was just learning about "Spiritual Warfare," and I had a psychiatric patient in one of the exam rooms. Before I walked into the room, I prayed, "God let her see the Jesus in my eyes!" As I walked into the room and she saw me, she jumped off the exam table backward, shot halfway up the wall, and threw her arms up in front of her face and screamed, "YOUR EYES, YOUR EYES!" Wow! It was then I realized this spiritual warfare stuff is real. More about that later!

18: WORKING IN THE EMERGENCY DEPARTMENT

Another patient brought himself to the E.D., and he was sitting in an exam room waiting for treatment. I walked into the room and asked him, "What brings you to the emergency department?"

He replied, "I either just killed my ex-wife or I dreamed I did." He had a small cut over his left eye. It looked like it might have been caused by her nail as she fought him. Forensic science was not available during that time. If it had been they could have examined her nails to see if his skin was under them. I called the police and reported what he had said, and they had to go to the house; thankfully he had given me the address. I waited and waited and waited and called again and told them we would not be able to hold him IF he decided to leave our E.D.

After about three hours and two more phone calls, they finally arrived and arrested him. He had indeed tried to strangle his wife with a telephone cord, but she was still alive. So, they had to call an ambulance and have her taken to the closest emergency department. His two young children were in the room as he had attempted to strangle her. So the poor police had their hands full, and that is why it took them so long to respond to my calls. It was also their first attempted murder case in their city. They had to help the two young boys who had experienced this tragedy. So that was also understandable as to why they took so long to respond to my calls. Cops and nurses get along well because of the stress of their jobs, and we always try to support one another.

His wife lived over the next year in a vegetative state with a tracheostomy tube to help her breathe. The facility where she was cared for brought her to us a few times over that year, as she needed to have tracheostomy care.

Her husband was arrested for attempted murder that same day he had attacked her. She lived a little over a year. We learned that if she died past a year, he would not be tried for murder. I had to go to his trial and point him out. That was a bit scary as I had my nurse's uniform and cap on, and he knew who I was.

When I returned home from the trial, I noticed what looked like a bullet hole in my bedroom window. However, it turns out it was caused by a rock that flew from the lawnmower as my husband mowed the lawn. WHEW! Guess my imagination was on high alert! But thankfully nothing ever happened to me.

The police, paramedics, and nurses always had a close bond due to the nature of our jobs. I have a high respect for all of them. I could never have been a cop! And a cop probably never could have been a nurse.

Which brings me to another emergency department story about a cop. He was assigned to stay with a patient being treated. I don't know what the patient had done, but he was under surveillance by a cop, so it probably wasn't good. As I prepared the syringe to give the patient a tetanus shot, I looked over and saw this brave cop turn white and pass out. I now had to care for two patients. Over the years, every time I saw him, we both had a laugh about that memory.

Another story was of our dear, old, retired surgeon, who was one of our emergency department docs. One day

18: WORKING IN THE EMERGENCY DEPARTMENT

he was in an exam room and another patient started to "crash" in the x-ray department, right down the hall from us. So he tried to hurry out of the room to attend to the other patient. His foot somehow got into the "kick bucket" (a bucket with wheels on it). And he could not remove his foot from the bucket, so he had it attached to his foot all the way down the hall, and he kept kicking the kick bucket until he was finally able to get free. This is one time the doctor "kicked the bucket," and thankfully the patient did <u>not</u> "kick the bucket." It was hilarious! Nurses just gotta have FUN!

Another funny story about this Doc. One time he was in an exam room, and he had two stethoscopes, one in his pocket and one around his neck. As he tried to listen to a patient's heartbeat, he had the end of stethoscope in his pocket on the patient's heart. But he had the one around his neck in his ears, and he kept tapping the one in his ears around his neck, not knowing why he could not hear the patient's heartbeat! We had quite a laugh over that one.

Now don't get nervous about going to the emergency department as the docs are all well trained in trauma care. And this older guy was really an excellent doctor, and we all loved him! He was the best! RIP, "Goldie," we love you!

I also learned early on you always must leave yourself an "out." One time we had a psychiatric patient, and he started chasing another nurse and me. She ran where there was no exit. Bad idea! I ran the other way and was finally able to distract him so she was not injured. Always leave yourself a way out!

One time the emergency department nurses and paramedics had a "meeting" at a local bar. My other friend, also a nurse, had to drive me home because I had imbibed a bit too much alcohol. As she drove into our driveway, my new "forever husband," whom she had never met before, came out of the house to meet us. The alcohol had really hit me by then, and I started to throw up. His first reaction was "DON'T LET HER THROW UP ON MY NEW TIRES!" Needless to say, she was not impressed with their first meeting. However, over the years, we all became great friends, and she decided he was a great guy after all. And that he is!

A book that impressed me greatly as an adult was *Abandonment to Divine Providence* by Rev. Jean-Pierre De Caussade. It was all about living in the present moment. Working in the emergency department taught me this lesson.

I was the nurse that usually went with the doctor when he had to talk to family members about the death of their loved one. I liked to comfort the family just by being there and trying to support them when the doctor had to give "bad news" to family members. I probably would have been a good hospice nurse. But the emergency department was definitely my "cup of tea" for twenty years. Every day was a new day and brought new patients into the hospital needing our help. There was "never a dull moment" in the E.D. as each day was packed with excitement and never boring. We did have our "frequent flyers" though, meaning those who come to the E.D. often. And of course, our "drug seekers" too.

18: WORKING IN THE EMERGENCY DEPARTMENT

Looking back on my many experiences, I realize now GOD was with me every step of the way. I was just beginning to learn about Him. The E.D. brought me closer to God and taught me the "PRESENT MOMENT IS THE ONLY MOMENT WE CAN BE SURE OF!!!" If you remember that, each day and every moment of every day you will always "be ready" to meet your Maker.

One day I had a new, young, doctor working with us. He did NOT believe in restraining combative psychiatric patients. The police used to bring in many of our patients to be examined before we would send them to one of our "sister" hospitals that had a psychiatric floor for those who could not pay. Our hospital had a psychiatric floor for private paying patients only.

One day I had a "day from HELL!" I was the "charge nurse" that day, meaning I was responsible for the whole emergency department. The first psychiatric patient was a young girl. When her parents drove her to the hospital, she quickly jumped out of the car and tore off all her clothes and ran out naked into the area where the construction workers were building new doctors' offices. They got "quite a show" that day. I had to run out and give her a sedative shot before we could bring her into the hospital. The young new doc would not let me restrain her. For me, that was "strike one!" We only had two RNs and an orderly to care for everyone, and I was not happy about being "in charge" that day.

The second patient was from another country, and the police brought him in to be examined because he chanted on his lawn and acted very bizarre and scared people. He was quite combative. In the waiting room he crashed into the Christmas tree, knocked it over, and cut his back on a broken ornament. We finally were able to get him inside the E.D. He then decided he was going to leave and started bolting for the double doors. Thank God they were "breakaway doors," and he did not hurt himself before we were able to stop him from running out into the ambulance bay. Again, the new, young, doc would not allow us to restrain him. Strike two for me!

The third psych patient was a little old man who was very depressed. By this time the E.D. doc finally had "changed his tune" about restraints, and he told me to restrain him. As I applied the leather restraints, he peacefully put his arms out to have the straps applied. He was the only patient that day that did NOT need to be restrained. Strike three for me!

That day was the "final straw" for me, as I was concerned for the safety of my patients. I also decided I did not want to lose my nursing license if someone was injured because of not being restrained when they needed to be.

So I wrote a letter to the director of nursing apprising her of the potential of someone being seriously hurt because we did not have enough help. Patient care needed to improve in the emergency department.

The emergency department was always my "first love!" Each day was different and always kept us "on our toes!" I have several more stories I could share about different patients I cared for, but they are not for the "weak of heart" or anyone who does not like "blood and guts!" Hence, I shall pass on those stories.

18: WORKING IN THE EMERGENCY DEPARTMENT

I worked there for twenty years and loved it. I hope and pray I meet some of my previous patients in Heaven one day! PRAY FOR ME TO GET THERE! AMEN!

Shortly after this "day from Hell," I requested a transfer to the Same Day Surgery floor, A.K.A. "Outpatient Surgery." I was thinking I would be able to sit down to chart my nursing notes instead of running around the E.D. all day. Also, my nursing license would not be in jeopardy as much as it was in the E.D. So I transferred to Same Day Surgery. Even though it is called Same Day Surgery, we also had to prepare in-house patients from the surgical floors, but they returned to their floor where they came from after their surgery. So they went directly from the Recovery Room back to their floor. So even though we had to prepare the "in-house" patients for surgery, we did not have to take care of them after surgery.

Shortly after transferring to Same Day, one of the nurses told me they needed me to go to the "marking room." This is where the plastic surgeons "mark" their patients before surgery. As I and another nurse entered the room, there was a patient on a stretcher covered head to toe with a sheet. As I got close to the patient, his arm came out from under the sheet, and he started saying "O' baby, baby" and making very inappropriate remarks as he tried to grope me. Well, I had had enough of this kind of shenanigans from working in the emergency department, so I said, "Nope, not going to deal with this!" And I started to leave the room. Then the "patient" pulled down the sheet covering his face and body. It was a fellow nurse, and he was playing a joke on me because it was APRIL FOOL'S DAY! Nurses just gotta have fun!

Not too long after I had transferred, the Director of Nursing, the one that I had written a letter to about patient care in the E.D., gave the emergency department another nurse. A triage nurse who was able to see patients and evaluate them before they were seen inside the E.D. They also made a special room for combative psychiatric patients that had padded walls so a person could not injure themselves. This would have been a great help when I was there, but at least it was a safer patient care environment now. So I felt better about that, even though I had already transferred to the Same Day Surgery Department.

I think one of my favorite stories about working in Same Day Surgery was the day I had prepared a lady to go to surgery for a D&C. We always had to do pregnancy tests on our female patients, and her test was POSITIVE! So, when the OR nurses came out to get her, I said, "NO! You cannot take her back to surgery." Then the doctor arrived, and I pulled him aside and told him the results. He then cancelled her surgery and spoke with the lady and her husband as I stood by. About a year later I received a letter from the baby's dad. He thanked me for saving his baby girl. And said she is such a JOY to them, and he could not thank me enough. Of course, I think any nurse would have done the same. But it was wonderful hearing from him and how happy they were with their little baby girl.

And now back to Same Day Surgery for a final story. My last patient was a sweet little old lady who was "deaf as a

18: WORKING IN THE EMERGENCY DEPARTMENT

door nail." I was doing the pre-op interview. She and her husband came into the room. He answered all the questions we always had to ask anyone going to surgery the next day.

As I spoke with him, he shared with me he was a retired neurological doctor who had worked at the same hospital where I had started my nursing career in NYC so many years before. We did not know each other then. He was originally from Lima, Peru where I had been an exchange student when I was seventeen.

I felt like this was a "complete circle" for me. The last thing he said to me, as we saw each other again as I was leaving the hospital, was "You need to tell your charge nurse that you are a wonderful nurse!" Wow, what a nice way to go out the door for the last time... full circle. I worked for a total of forty-three years as an RN and have no regrets as it was a "great ride."

Always remember the "present moment is the only moment we can be sure of!" Think about that for a moment!!

19

ADOPTION OF MY BEAUTIFUL BABY DAUGHTER

Remember my story of being an exchange student in high school? Well, one day I received a call from one of our high school exchange students. His name was Sergio, and he lived in Colombia, and many years had passed since I had contact with him. He asked me if he could come to Florida to visit me. Of course, I said "YES!!"

During his visit we went to a Burger King on Federal Highway in Pompano Beach. After we had gotten our food, I looked up and saw a redheaded girl enter the restaurant. I poked him and said, "I think she is from Colombia, and I am going to go talk to her."

He said to me, "<u>You are crazy</u>!"

And so I did go and talk to her, and I invited her to sit and have lunch with us. She had walked there that day, and she and her husband owned a condo on the beach. We talked, and after eating our lunch, I told her I would drive her home as it was a very hot day, and so I did. We

19: ADOPTION OF MY BEAUTIFUL BABY

exchanged phone numbers, and this began a long friendship. Sergio returned to Colombia, and I have since lost contact with him, so he has no idea of what transpired after he returned to Colombia.

Remember my prize speaking class in ninth grade, when I had recited an article at Regionals called "Someday Maria?" I had read it in a *Guidepost Magazine* written by Eddie Albert, the actor in the TV show called *Green Acres*. It was about how he and his wife had adopted a little girl from Spain. Well, this "planted a seed in my heart" to adopt a baby from another country someday. After a few years I mentioned to my Colombian friend I had always wanted to adopt a baby from another country. Her reply was, "My mother is best friends with the lady in charge of adoptions in our city in Colombia!" And as they say, "the rest is history!"

Now, the following is the story of what we had to go through to adopt my baby girl. My friend had translated all the paperwork and sent it to the adoption agency in Colombia. They replied to me saying the paperwork must be officially/legally translated and stamped. So this delayed us longer. We also had to be fingerprinted and go through a home-study by Immigration in Miami. We did all this and sent everything to the adoption agency in Colombia.

Then the waiting began. We waited and waited and finally I could not wait any longer! So one day I flipped open the Yellow Pages and found a ham radio operator in Hollywood Beach, Florida. I called him and told him my story and asked him to contact another ham radio operator in Colombia. He did this, and then the ham radio operator in Bogota made a phone call to the adoption agency in Ibague. So we had a four-way conversation between two ham radio operators, the lawyer on the phone, and me on the phone. The "final answer" from the lawyer was, "YES, come NOW because I am going on vacation in a few weeks!"

Fortunately, we already had our passports ready and quickly got the plane tickets. When we arrived in Bogota, we had no idea where to stay. But fortunately, we had met a man on the plane, he was very helpful, and he told us what hotel to go to in Bogota. He was an American businessman, and he "took us under his wing." He told us he would come to our room the next morning and help us get to the city where our baby was. And so early the next morning he knocked on our door and helped us so much. I never knew his name, but once again God was looking out for us. And I thank God for him!

He took us to the place where we could catch a bus to the city where our baby was. Now, THAT was quite a trip. There were chickens and pigs on top of the bus. As we drove along on a very narrow road cars came straight at us, and at the very last minute, they swerved to miss hitting the bus. On the right side of the road was a very steep and deep ravine with a river flowing below. On the other side of the road was a very high mountain, and the roads were tortuous, narrow, and very dangerous.

My friend's mother had chosen our baby out of all the children in the orphanage, and she visited her every day

19: ADOPTION OF MY BEAUTIFUL BABY

until we arrived. She also bought her clothes to wear and gave her lots of loving care. We arrived at the orphanage and met our beautiful baby girl; she was only two months old. So if we had not been delayed with the paperwork, we might not have gotten her; it might have been a different baby. God again was looking over all of us.

Usually, they do not allow the future parents to take a baby until all the legal paperwork is final. But they did let us take her the same day because we stayed in my friend's mom's home. The next day we returned to complete all the legal paperwork. A couple from the Peace Corp., who had also adopted a baby, were the witnesses to our baby girl's adoption and signed the legal paperwork.

I remember scrubbing my baby's cloth diapers on a stone washboard at the home of my friend's mom. It was also interesting to learn the baby formula was made in the USA and consisted of powdered milk made by Borden's.

I also remember thinking I was going to die in Colombia because I had "Montezuma's Revenge" for several days. A memory I would like to forget!

So if I had not listened to my "inner prompting" that day in Burger King so many years ago, I would never have adopted my beautiful baby girl. I named her Connie (named after my mom) Ann, and she was my "Bicentennial Baby."

After we had completed all the legal paperwork, we were able to return to Bogota. Now, that was a memorable trip too. It was night, and we drove in a collectivo, which is the equivalent to a taxi; there were two strangers in the car with us. They sat in the front seat with the driver, and we were in the backseat with the baby. It was cold in the mountains, and it had been raining. Suddenly, a horse's rear end came through the windshield! Glass flew all over, but thankfully no one was injured. We jumped out of the car, and I was still holding the baby. I stood in mud up to my knees; because of all the rain there had been mud slides. I had to get out of the way quickly as we were on a curve and were afraid of being hit by another car if it came around the bend.

It just so happened we were in a small town. Someone came out with a broom and brushed all the glass off where the windshield had been, and on we went with the cold wind blowing on us all the way to Bogota.

When we arrived in Bogota, the couple who could speak Spanish disappeared into the crowd. The driver was in jeopardy of losing his job as his boss did not believe him when he shared the story of what had happened. So little old me had to explain, in my very broken Spanish, what had happened. I said, "Un caballo! BOOM," as I slapped my hands together! We were surrounded by several people all listening to my story of the accident. Everyone burst out laughing when I gave my explanation. But thankfully, it was enough for the driver to save his job, as his boss believed my story.

I called her my Bicentennial baby as it was 1976. She had a "close call" three times in her first year of life. The first was when she was two months old, and that story is above. The second "close call" was when we were back home, and she was in her walker with wheels on it. She had just left

19: ADOPTION OF MY BEAUTIFUL BABY

the kitchen when a glass coke bottle exploded, and glass flew all over the kitchen floor. And the third time she had just left the bathroom, and the ceiling crashed down onto the floor. She was, and still is, a blessed baby! God was looking out for her too and still is today.

When she was thirteen, I dragged her to the Youth Group at our Church. She was not happy with me! I introduced her to the leader, and when I went back an hour and a half later, she was all smiles. She loved Youth Group and still has lifelong friends from those teenage years. She has a beautiful voice, and as a teen she sang in the youth choir and the choir for Mass. The area where she was born in Colombia is noted for their musical talents.

If I had not listened to my "inner prompting" that day in Burger King so many years ago, I would never have adopted my beautiful baby girl.

Now it is "confession time" as the best thing that came out of my first marriage was the adoption of my baby girl. We divorced when she was very young.

Our daughter is now married to a great guy, and they have three beautiful children. She is a school counselor, and her husband is an "IT" guy.

20

MY "FOREVER HUSBAND"

When I returned to college, I met my future "forever husband" in Speech Class. He gave a speech about how to pack a suitcase, and when he pulled out some purple underwear, everyone roared with laughter! He is the worst suitcase packer now. If we are going somewhere, he takes his clothes and throws them into his suitcase on the morning we are leaving!

When my daughter was five years old, I got pregnant and had a baby boy named Matthew, which means "Gift of God!" And he surely is that.

Matthew was also very active in Youth Group at our Church, and he played the bass guitar in a band with his friends. He stays in contact with the others in his Youth Group also. He is married to a great gal; she is a professional photographer and specializes in underwater photography as well as other types of photography. Her business is called "O.S.W. Images, One Sweet World Images." They have twins, a boy and a girl, and they are a blessing to us. They live in Texas.

20: MY "FOREVER HUSBAND"

Our son Matthew was in the Air Force, and he followed in his grandfather's and his dad's footsteps. He now has a good job because of what he learned in the U.S.A.F.

Once again God is good all the time... all the time God is good!

I hope you are still with me! Hang in there; the best is yet to come....

21

A GLASS OF ICE WATER! THE BEGINNING OF MY CONVERSION TO THE CATHOLIC FAITH

Wow, where do I begin?! I had attended a non-denominational Church at one time. I also had several Protestant friends, and we would pray together. I loved the praise and worship and still do. Remember my ma playing Gospel music on the radio when I was a kid? It is still in my blood! Tennessee Ernie and Jim Reeves always get me praising our Lord! I love Country Gospel music!

To make a very long story short, it turns out my future "forever husband" was a CATHOLIC! And his whole family including four siblings were all CATHOLIC! We dated and he did NOT "dump me," like my first encounter with the Catholic guy back in nursing school.

In fact, we were married, however not in the Catholic Church originally. The first time we were married was in a

21: A GLASS OF ICE WATER!

Cessna Airplane at 7,000 feet above sea level over Delray Beach, Fl. where my husband worked as a UPS driver. We were married by a Jewish Justice of the Peace, and a friend of mine, also an RN, was the maid of honor. Connie was the "flower girl" in the plane. The pilot was my instructor from a class I had taken years earlier called "Aviation Ground School." The guys in the tower joked about how they should have attached tin cans to the plane.

The pilot and the maid of honor fell in love and were married a few years later. He took us flying on our anniversary for a few years after we were married. Until he had a heart attack, and we then decided maybe we should not carry on the tradition! The second time we were married by a Methodist minister because the Baptist minister was on vacation. We were married on the "Top Lot." Remember when I was eight years old, and I mentioned the "Top Lot" the first time? Our families were not able to come to the first wedding because the Cessna airplane was too small! There will be much more about the "Top Lot" a little later. The local people call it the "altar!"

Yes, my husband was a Catholic, but he never pushed me to convert, and he never said we should have been married in the Catholic Church because he was Catholic. Who knew? Not me! He probably knew I would have "headed for the hills" if he had tried to get me to become a Catholic. I was very anti-Catholic at the time!

Now, to digress a bit, when my daughter was three years old, she attended a Baptist pre-school. One day she brought a book home called *Christian Living in the Home*, and it was about having your husband be the leader of the household, or the "head" of the household. I remember the first two times I read it I tossed it aside and I said, "NO WAY!" The third time, after my marriage to my "forever husband," I decided to try their advice.

My "forever hubby" and I attended a Catholic Church together. I used to go home every Sunday and cry all afternoon. Because I wanted to sing praises to God and sing Hallelujah, but I had to sit on my hands at Mass to keep from raising them in praise. The priest was a young, newly ordained priest, and he gave great homilies. He would always tell a joke during his homilies. Well, hubby and I would be the only ones who would laugh at his jokes! The "Frozen Chosen," a name I had heard about "typical" Catholics, and it seemed to be true, at least at that Church.

One day my husband asked me if I would be willing to have this priest come to our home and talk to me about our two children being baptized? When I knew my husband wanted the kids baptized, I decided that I wanted to be baptized too, BUT NOT CATHOLIC! I was afraid if I let our kids be baptized Catholic, they would go to Hell and so would I for allowing it. That is how anti-Catholic I was at the time. So I made arrangements with my pa to have the Baptist minister from the First Baptist Church baptize me in our beautiful Lake in the boonies of NY. So I had a total immersion baptism in the lake I loved. My daughter sang two beautiful songs, "AMEN" and "Seek yea first the Kingdom of God!"

21: A GLASS OF ICE WATER!

I did finally agree to have the Catholic priest come to our home. So after Mass one Sunday he came over. We sat around the kitchen table and talked. He and I had a great time, laughing and sharing. After three hours I gave him a GLASS OF ICE WATER! Can you believe it? No food, just a GLASS OF ICE WATER!

That day we were both so happy, and he practically skipped to his car. He asked me, "Is it OK if I come back next Sunday?"

I replied, "Of course."

And so return he did. After another two and a half hours and another glass of ice water, he recommended we go to a nearby Charismatic Catholic Church. He knew I was used to a Non-Denominational Protestant Church where they worshiped more than a typical Catholic Church. He knew it was a Catholic Church and that would satisfy my husband, and he knew they used lots of praise and worship, and that would make me happy.

I told him he and my husband would both be "six feet under" before I ever became a Catholic! I said it nicely though! Then he said, "Too late, honey; you already are Catholic. You just don't know it yet! You are more Catholic than 99 percent of my parishioners!" I was not thrilled by this news. But we took his advice and transferred to a very charismatic Catholic Church.

One day, after many years had passed and I had finally started the Rite of Christian Initiation for Adults (RCIA) program to enter the Catholic Church. I realized I wanted to try to find the priest who had sent us to the Charismatic

Catholic Church because I wanted to tell him it was because of him I was becoming a Catholic! I had no idea how to find a priest. But God knew!

A day or two after I had the thought of trying to find him, I went to work in same day surgery. I worked on the pre-op side getting patients ready for surgery. For some reason, I walked over to the "post-op" side. And there was this priest lying on a stretcher. He was a "pre-op" patient, but for some reason he was on the "post-op" side. Maybe we had too many patients on the "pre-op" side? Anyway, I saw him and was amazed! I went up to him, and I said, "Father, do you remember me?"

He said, "YES, I remember YOU, but I don't remember your name!"

I then proceeded to tell him the story of how I had wanted to reach him but did not know how to do so. When he heard this, the hair on his arms stood straight up as did mine! We both knew without a doubt God had put us together once again! Another **GOD**cidence, it was a mini miracle he was having surgery at my hospital. Usually, priests go to the Catholic hospital down the street.

And now there is more.... It "just so happened" he was ready to be discharged when I was ready to go home. So I offered to take him to the Church where I started my journey to the Catholic Church, where his mom, who was still the housekeeper there, would be able to care for him. As we walked into the rectory (place where the priests live) there was another priest who came in from the garden. He was in overalls covered in mud. So the priest who had had

21: A GLASS OF ICE WATER!

the surgery introduced me to the pastor of the Church, and we sent the priest off to bed to recuperate. When the other priest found out I was in the RCIA (Rite of Christian Initiation for Adults) program and learning to become a Catholic, he was excited. He told me he used to teach RCIA, and he wanted to show me his recently built new Church. It was also beginning to rain. But he said, "Let's go!"

And so we walked in the rain over to his new Church. He then proceeded to show me every stained-glass window and explained what each window meant. WOW! What a blessing for me to have a pastor of the Church take the time to do all of this for me! It was another GODcidence! I call these "events" GODcidences instead of coincidences because God is the one doing all these amazing things for me.

The night our son, Matthew, received the Sacrament of Confirmation, the bishop and a priest were processing down the aisle. Another GODcidence happened as the priest with the bishop was the same priest that had sent us to this Charismatic Catholic Church. Afterward I went up to him to tell him it was because of him Matthew was being confirmed, as he had sent us to this Charismatic Church. Then, here comes the GODcidence part.... He told me that he was not supposed to be there that night. The priest assigned to accompany the bishop was sick. The priest had called him to ask him if he could take his place. Praise God!

And over the years, God kept placing him in my path at unexpected times. The last time was after we attended a Mass at the Church near the cemetery. After Mass, I told my husband I wanted to stop at the priest's cemetery, and after a short while, a car pulled up and the same priest, who was now an auxiliary bishop, got out of the car and walked up to us. I told him I prayed for him to become the bishop in New York State, where the priests retreat will be someday! He laughed and said, "If that happens, I would not like the cold!" Unbeknownst to us at the time... he was soon assigned as a bishop in Florida.

22

CONVERSION OF A VERY PROTESTING PROTESTANT INTO THE CATHOLIC FAITH

At this new Catholic Church, I attended the Monday night prayer group. And I would "beg God to show me the TRUTH; did HE want me to become a Catholic?" I was very anti-Catholic at the time, and He would have to show me Himself because I was so stubborn and prideful, I would not listen to anyone else. I could relate to Saint Paul BEFORE he converted; I used to think like a mini-Saul.

Then, one night at intercessory prayer, I had what I call a "movie in my mind." First, I will share what I saw, and then I will follow it with what it all meant. I saw a HUGE fish; its tail was at the ceiling and its head was at the floor. As I watched, the scales of the fish began to fall off onto the floor. Behind the scales was pure white meat. Then the meat opened up and inside was a Crucifix.

Now for the meaning of it all, which came to me in an instant: the fish was a mackerel as my father had always spoken of the Catholics as "mackerel snatchers" as they always ate fish on Fridays back then. God surely has a sense of humor! The scales falling off the fish meant two things:

1) The scales represented all the "garbage" I had always heard about the Catholic Church.
2) The scales were falling off my eyes.
3) Pure white meat meant the purity of the Church, you had to dig deep, you had to read a lot, pray a lot, and you had to study a lot about the lives of the Saints to see the purity of the Church.
4) Then when the white meat opened, and the crucifix was deep inside, my reaction was "Oh no, I have to become a Catholic!" The Protestant Churches do NOT have Jesus on the cross. The Catholics do, as a constant reminder Jesus loves us so much, He was willing to do His Father's will and die for us, for our redemption, so that we could spend eternity with Him in Heaven.

I had a Protestant tell me one time he thought Catholics did not believe in the Resurrection because we keep Him on the cross. Of course, we DO believe in His Resurrection!

22: CONVERSION OF A VERY PROTESTING

And that "movie in my mind" was the beginning of my conversion into the Catholic Church. I knew God wanted me to become a Catholic.

I began by taking classes called the RCIA (Rite of Christian Initiation for Adults) program. I had a very difficult time in this class as I was still a very "protesting Protestant." But I knew God wanted me to become a Catholic, so I had to PERSEVERE!

My sponsor was a very rotund man who used to stand in the doorway every Monday night, with his big belly taking up the whole door and his arms crossed. Sponsors are only required to attend classes once a month, but he was there EVERY MONDAY NIGHT. He probably knew I would bolt for the door if he wasn't standing in the doorway. After every class he would spend another thirty minutes or more answering all my many questions.

My "forever husband" could not be my sponsor because of his job, as he worked late every day.

23

HOW I CAME TO BELIEVE IN THE IN THE MOST HOLY EUCHARIST

"If we but paused for a moment to consider attentively what takes place in this Sacrament of the Eucharist, I am sure that the thought of Christ's love for us would transform the coldness of our hearts into a fire of love and gratitude."
—*St. Teresa of Avila (Teresa of Jesus)*

So finally, after being at this Charismatic Church since the mid-eighties, after much procrastination, it came time for the "Rite of Sending" where those in the RCIA class would go to meet the bishop. We had our annual rally the night before, and the priest said, "If anyone needs prayer for anything, ask the person next to you to pray for you." My husband ushered, and not next to me. So I asked this complete stranger to pray for me.

23: HOW I CAME TO BELIEVE

My dilemma was this: I did not want to meet the Bishop because I did not believe that Jesus was truly ALIVE in the Eucharist. I did not want to be a hypocrite. So this stranger prayed over me, and I went home and went to sleep.

I awoke at 5 a.m., and I had had a vivid dream. I had seen an oval shaped glass bowl full of water. Floating in the water was what looked like a white ravioli. As I looked at the object, I could see that it was beating, "Thump, thump." "Thump, thump." "Thump, thump." Then the bowl broke open, and the "ravioli" broke into hundreds of pieces on the altar. Each piece was still beating, "thump, thump," "thump, thump," "thump, thump!" Then a dark-skinned, hairy forearm came down from above and picked up each piece. They were all still beating. Then he gave each piece to the people who came forward to receive.

The interpretation of this dream came to me as I awoke. The water in the bowl was the living water of Christ. The "ravioli" was the Eucharist, and it was the beating heart of Christ; it was beating "thump, thump" to show me HE IS ALIVE IN THE MOST HOLY EUCHARIST! The "ravioli" was to show me it had substance. When it fell onto the altar, it broke into many pieces, and each piece still beat, meaning HE IS ALIVE. Then the pieces together formed a large heart, and each piece still beat individually. The dark arm coming down from Heaven was the arm of Jesus. The priest is in persona Christi. Praise GOD!

So, I went off to meet the Bishop with much JOY in my heart. And several months later I entered the Catholic Church on the Easter Vigil on March 30, 1991. And this was marriage number three as we had our marriage blessed by the Catholic Church that night. To God be all the Glory! More explanation in the next chapter!

For anyone thinking about leaving the Catholic Church my advice is this.... IF you truly believe Jesus is ALIVE in the Most Holy Eucharist, please reconsider leaving. HE IS ALIVE IN THE EUCHARIST: Body, Blood, Soul, and Divinity, and if you leave, then you are leaving Jesus behind. Unfortunately, 70 percent of Catholics do not believe that Jesus is ALIVE in the Eucharist!

The institution of the Eucharist and the priesthood both occurred at the Last Supper. Because of "Apostolic Succession," the priesthood in the Catholic Church is present from the time of Jesus.

Stay tuned, you won't want to miss this one....

24

MY ENTRANCE INTO THE CATHOLIC CHURCH AND MY LIFE'S MISSION

"If you learn everything except Christ, you learn nothing.
"If you learn nothing except Christ, you learn everything."
—St. Bonaventure

"Start by doing what is necessary. Then do what is possible. Suddenly you will be doing the impossible."
—St. Francis of Assisi

When I was preparing to marry my "forever husband" on the night I was to enter the Catholic Church, I was able to move forward because I remembered how my first husband used to say he was baptized a Catholic. I was able to track down a secretary from the Diocese where he had been born, and she searched and searched and finally was able to find his wrongly filed Baptismal certificate. She found the proper paperwork about two weeks before I was due to enter the Catholic Church, and this proved he was baptized a Catholic. Once this was discovered, I was able to move forward because according to Catholic Church teachings, if you were Baptized Catholic, you must be married in the Catholic Church for it to be a valid marriage in the eyes of the Church. He was not, so I got off on what I called a "technicality!"

The deadline of the Easter Vigil was fast approaching, and I needed to have this paperwork to be able to enter the Catholic Church at the Easter Vigil and have my forever husband and my marriage blessed by the Church. And I was then able to be married to my CATHOLIC GUY, the one who never "dumped me!" So this was our marriage number three! Or marriage number one in the Catholic Church!

The night I entered the Catholic Church, March 30, 1991, right after receiving Jesus in the Most Holy Eucharist, I "heard" words in my heart. The words I heard, not with my ears, but deep within my heart were "WELCOME INTO MY KINGDOM IN A NEW AND MORE POWERFUL WAY, MY LITTLE CLOWN; I HAVE CALLED YOU TO HELP REBUILD MY CHURCH!" Whoa! I thought, "What is this? I become a Catholic and I start to go crazy?! I replied, "I will do whatever You want me to do Lord." I did not know what He wanted me to do. And so I prayed every day, for several months, "What do you want me to do Lord? I will do it!"

THEN one morning I awoke, and words and thoughts kept coming to my mind, so many I had to get up and

24: MY ENTRANCE INTO THE CATHOLIC CHURCH

write them all down. The "bottom line" is HE wants me (us) to build a retreat center for priests up on the "TOP LOT!" Remember the "Top Lot" when I was a little girl? The "Top Lot" where I had gotten married the second time to my Catholic husband? The same "Top Lot" my pa had given to us when we got married up there? It is fifteen acres of Heaven!

This has since become my LIFE'S MISSION, this and praying for HIS priest sons. My "Journey to the Top Lot" progressed.

Now a bit of spiritual advice about discernment: Whenever you think God is "talking to you," you must have it discerned. Number one: is this from me or You Lord? Number two: is it from Satan? Number three: is it from God? Well, I knew it certainly was NOT from me; helping priests was the last thing on my mind! Is it from Satan? Pretty sure he would NOT want to help God's priests in any way.

Number three: Is it from God? If it is from God, then IT WILL HAPPEN. I just need to have faith and get out of His way!

Over the years it has been confirmed many, many, times by different lay people, priests and even a bishop, that "YES, this is from God!"

These were similar words Saint Francis of Assisi "heard" when he prayed before the San Damiano cross in the Portiuncula, a small broken-down chapel. The story of St. Francis is one everyone should read. I did not know about these words or about St. Francis of Assisi when I "heard" these words in my heart. I know now we are ALL "called to help rebuild His Church."

We all have a purpose in life, and HE knows what it is; all we must do is beg him to show us what HE wants us to do with our lives? How does HE want us to rebuild HIS Church?

25

THE "TOP LOT" IS GOD'S HOLY MOUNTAIN OF FAITH

One day I heard these words in my heart, and I realized faith meant two things regarding the Top Lot. One is it will be a place where our priests will have their faith renewed. And two it will take much faith on my part to put God's plan into action. I have been waiting and praying since 1991. May God's will be done in His time and not mine.

It will be a place where a priest can rest his weary head in one of our hermitages. And he will be renewed as he walks in God's country. He will come closer to God and will be filled with the Holy Spirit as he is renewed by Him.

This project will take the prayers and donations of many. When I first received this whole "Grand Plan" I knew we are supposed to build hermitages so that each priest will be able to be alone with God. Originally, I received we were to build twelve hermitages. We will start with one and go from there. When we met with our local bishop, he also mentioned hermitages, which was a confirmation for me.

After learning about how God spoke to St. Francis from the San Damiano Cross, I knew I had to investigate the Secular Franciscan Order, now called the OFS, or Order of Franciscans Secular. I started classes to enter this order. And after a few years of study, I was professed a Secular Franciscan on Nov. 19, 1999. Hurricane Irene prevented me from being professed the month earlier.

After several more years I was first elected the Vice Minister of St. Anthony of Padua Secular Franciscan Order in Boynton Beach, Florida for two three-year terms. Then I was elected their minister for two more three-year terms for a total of twelve years. That was a learning experience for me, and of course it was a humbling experience too. I thank God for our spiritual assistant, Fr. Tom Murphy OFM, as whenever we had a visitation, which is when our regional spiritual assistant visits our fraternity and reviews the records and actions of our fraternity, he would sit next to me and keep me calm. He has been one of my mentors over the years and always encourages me. I thank God for him daily. He has written a book titled *A Pater Noster Psalter, Praying the Psalms in the Light of The Lord's Prayer* (using the *Revised Grail Psalms* written by Rev. Thomas K. Murphy OFM and Mrs. Pamela Nagle, OFS).

I never told my pa, the AMERICAN BAPTIST, I had entered the Catholic Church because I was afraid to. However, I found out a few years later he knew my secret. He had lymphoma, and he came to visit us in Florida. While visiting, I took him for his radiation treatments at a

25: THE "TOP LOT" IS GOD'S HOLY

Catholic hospital. At the registration desk, they always ask you your religion. I almost groaned when Poppa said, "I'm a Baptist, An AMERICAN BAPTIST," as he slapped his hand on the desk. Then he said, "I have a son that's a Methodist, a daughter that's a Catholic (he said it nicely though!), and another son that's a nothing!" The "nothing" son later began attending the Baptist Church again. May his soul rest in peace.

I figured out Pa must have put two and two together when I asked him for my baptismal certificate from the First Baptist Church. He must have known I was "up to something!" Interesting note: the Catholic Church accepts a Protestant baptism, but the Protestant Church does not accept a Catholic baptism.

Years later, he was on his death bed in the farmhouse where my brothers and I grew up. I stayed next to him twenty-four hours a day until he passed to eternal life. I waited until he was in a coma before I prayed the "Three Prayers for the Dying" from the Pieta book. I was afraid to pray them while he was still alert as I thought it would upset him to have Catholic prayers prayed for him. I prayed these every day until on the third day he passed to eternal life. Rest in peace, Poppa! Then I prayed for his soul in purgatory. I knew he did not believe in purgatory, but I sure do. I still pray for him at every Mass and for all my family members who have passed to eternal life.

When my oldest brother, Bill, was dying of cancer, my other brother Don and his wife and my husband drove to see him about two weeks before he died. The night before

I was to leave for home, he came to me in their kitchen. I had my back to him as I washed dishes in the sink. He said to me, "Unlike you Catholics who have to go to purgatory, I am going straight up!"

Without missing a beat, I said, "Just because you don't believe it doesn't mean it isn't so!" And for the first time in his life, he had no reply. But the next morning he came to me in the kitchen again, and we were face to face.

He then said, "I have friends who are Catholic, and I know when someone dies, they have a Mass for them. So, IF you want to, you can have one said for me." So maybe he thought about what I had said the night before, and he wanted to "cover all bases!" RIP, brother Bill.

After he died, I did have a Mass for him, and I continue to pray for the repose of his soul and all members of my family at every Mass, those living and all those who have passed to eternal life.

This is the same brother my parents had given the task of teaching me how to slow dance at the age of thirteen. I remember him constantly yelling at me to "STOP LEADING!" And to this very day I still try to "lead" whenever I slow dance with my hubby!

Since God led me into the Catholic Church, I have been a "leader" of the Secular Franciscans, a leader of the Extraordinary Ministers of Holy Communion, and the founder/leader of the Sonlight Clown Ministry. God also led me to become a lector and a sacristan. Lots of leading, but following Christ is much more important than any leading I ever did. Amen!

25: THE "TOP LOT" IS GOD'S HOLY

GOD LEADS IF YOU LISTEN! Be still and LISTEN and HE will "speak to your heart too." And if HE calls you into leadership, then do it and be not afraid.

God did not say it would be easy! After I had "heard" Him speak to my heart the night I entered the Catholic Church, I had a "tough row to hoe!"

My first obstacle to moving forward with the "Top Lot Ministry for priests" was my dear CATHOLIC husband. Over many years of my hearing, "HOW DO YOU KNOW IT'S FROM GOD?" And after many years of my many prayers to Heaven, we were standing in the kitchen of our old farmhouse when I said to him, "LET'S ASK HIM!" And so I prayed a short prayer for God to confirm this whole "GRAND PLAN" for him!" Then I "felt led" to open the door to Auntie FranCies' room, the first Catholic I had known. She is the one I used to listen to Archbishop Fulton Sheen on the radio with, when I was eight years old, remember? She had long ago passed to eternal life, but I knew she still prayed for me.

So upon entering her room I looked up high on a shelf, and there was something wrapped in brown butcher paper. It had writing on it, something about "The Blessed Virgin Mary," and so I asked my dear doubting husband to "please take that down for me." Well, he did! And as I opened the butcher paper, I discovered several VERY OLD magazines, written in the late 1800s. There were about twenty-three magazines and I reached in and pulled out ONE magazine. I opened the first page, and it had a list of many priests, bishops and mother superiors (founders of nuns) on the first page. NOT ONE OF THE OTHER magazines had these names in them! That was the start of my Catholic husband beginning to believe, yes, this was from God!

Another "eye opener" for him was one day on Palm Sunday back in 1999 we had returned from Church, and I decided to make our first pamphlet for the "Top Lot." I copied and pasted some of the photos I had taken over the years. He just happened to enter the den as I worked on this pamphlet. He looked at one of the photos and said, "That looks like Jesus in the fire!" And he was right; you could see him in the fire, and this photo has been confirmed by many others over the years. I have had two different photos showing Jesus in the fire! I think God is showing people this so they will get "ON FIRE" to help us make this a physical reality too.

Now that we are both retired, I am still waiting... sometimes not so patiently. I still feel like a donkey with a carrot in front of my nose. Every time I begin to feel a little discouraged about when will it ever happen, a priest will call or a lay person will call or give me an encouraging word or a donation. Then the carrot is pulled out a few more inches, and I must keep moving forward to "reach the carrot!" THEN I REMEMBER MY CHILDHOOD EXPERIENCES WITH PERSEVERANCE... NEVER GIVE UP!

One time we had a dear Franciscan priest, Fr. Julio, stay at our parish for a few years. I had asked him if he would help me and be my spiritual assistant. He agreed and we met once a month in his office. He always sat across his

25: THE "TOP LOT" IS GOD'S HOLY

desk, and he always prayed silently with his eyes closed. I had shared my whole story about the night I entered the Church and all the rest of the story about the "Top Lot."

Then one day I said to him, "Father, do you think this will ever happen in my lifetime?"

As he sat across his desk with his eyes closed, I knew he prayed, and after a few moments, he gently shook his head up and down, and he said, "YES, IT WILL HAPPEN IN YOUR LIFETIME!"

Then I replied, "Does that mean I have to live to be 150?"

He bowed his head again and with eyes closed I could see a slight smile cross his face as he then said, "Hummmm, maybe 200!" Gotta love those Holy Spirit filled Franciscan priests!

He wrote a book called *Encounters with the Holy Spirit*. It is a testimony of his childhood, adult life, and his priesthood, by Fr. Julio Rivero TOR. It is a wonderful book of his life and how God used him to help others. God continues to use Father to help others.

I attended one of his Masses at a Carmelite Monastery one time. At that Mass, I sensed I was to pray, "Jesus I trust in You times three, and Thy will be done times three." This has become one of my favorite prayers now.

26

SPIRITUAL WARFARE AND INTERCESSORY PRAYER THE GOOD AND THE BAD

Regarding spiritual warfare, I will not go into any details of our experiences. I will just give you a word of advice. Just BE CAREFUL! Don't go off on your own or with a group unless you are under the care of a priest that knows about spiritual warfare. It is easy for some in the group, even the leaders, to be deceived and can lead to many problems in a parish and in people's lives. It is also something that should not be shared. Be sure you are under the protection of a priest that knows about spiritual warfare or under the care of an exorcist in your Diocese or Archdiocese.

Good things can come from intercessory prayer too. One night during prayer, I got the "inner nudging" I was supposed to talk to a young fellow. I asked him "if he had ever discerned the priesthood?" He replied, "Yes, I am going to Omaha Nebraska to discern the priesthood next week!" So

26: SPIRITUAL WARFARE

this was confirmation for him he was supposed to discern the priesthood. He has since become a priest!

Now I know whenever I get the "inner nudging" that is the Holy Spirit talking to my soul, and I must act and trust in God. Several times since then I have sensed some young fellow might be being "called" to the priesthood. I ask them if anyone has ever mentioned that to them before. Then I tell them to pray about it and see if God "speaks to their heart." And if he does, then they need to discern it with their priest or with the help of a vocation director.

One night as the leaders of the intercessory prayer group prayed and shared what they thought God was showing them, I had a "movie in my mind." I saw a large white movie screen with blood dripping down onto the screen. It caused me to look up to see where the blood came from. As I looked UP I saw Jesus above the white screen. And it "came to me" that we must LOOK UP TO JESUS and <u>not</u> be so focused on the "visions" or what we thought we saw. Everything must be discerned, and we must not just believe everything is from Him. Discernment is a gift we all need. Our focus should be on GOD, not our visions. It is easy to be led astray if we do not focus on HIM.

27

THE SONLIGHT CLOWN MINISTRY

After several years of attending this Catholic Church, I wanted to start a clown ministry. Using a play on words, it was named the <u>Son</u>Light Clown Ministry. Son meaning Jesus, instead of the SUN.

In our "hay day" we had twenty-seven clowns. It was great fun bringing the JOY of Jesus to so many people. We even evangelized on the beach one day. Of course, we also got kicked off the beach by the cops as evidently evangelizing on the beach was illegal. Who knew? Not me! It was a great day as we met so many people happy we were there. We handed out scripture verses and spoke with many children and adults. And took some great photos of one of our clowns, BONGO, playing with a baby sitting in his car seat on the beach. The baby was smiling!

We also visited nursing homes. I took my miniature lop-eared bunny, Blessed Bunny, with us one day. As he sat in the lap of an elderly lady, she put her hands around

27: THE SONLIGHT CLOWN MINISTRY

Blessed Bunny's neck and started squeezing. We had to pry her hands off his neck to save his life! I did not know she suffered from dementia.

Another time we visited retirement homes behind another Catholic Church. At one of the private cottages an elderly lady opened the door. She was THRILLED we had come to visit as it was her ninety-first birthday and no one had visited her. We did not know it was her birthday. So we made her day when we sang happy birthday and made her flower balloons. Another <u>GOD</u>cidence! The purpose of our ministry was to bring the JOY OF JESUS to others.

We also went to a children's daycare one time. These little ones had never had the opportunity to see clowns. So that was a fun day for all. We painted the tiny faces there and at Church picnics and even at hospital picnics.

We also participated in the Fourth of July parade and handed out scripture verses to all those along the road. One year, we were invited to be in the Orange Bowl Parade. That was lots of fun.

One time "Animal Quackers" and "Tutti Frutti" were going to a meeting of the Ladies Guild with their priests from different Catholic Churches. When we arrived, we mistakenly entered the wrong room, where they were having a wedding reception. So without skipping a beat, we locked arms and marched through the room humming the tune to "Here Comes the Bride!" All the people at the reception and the bride and groom had a great laugh. Clowns just gotta have fun!

One of our skits was "The Calling of the Disciples." We preformed it for our bishop, and he loved it. We had twelve clowns preform and one "voice of God," A.K.A. "Waldo."

One time we had a "Night of JOY" at our Church. The music ministry sang lots of JOYFUL songs. One skit we did was the "Stagecoach Skit" performed by our son and his best friend. To end the night, we had a huge laundry basket filled with red clown noses. I announced to the crowd I was going to allow them to do something their parents never let them do as kids. Then I held the basket up and told them that they "COULD PICK THEIR NOSES!" That was great fun.

Some of our clown names were Doofy, Butterfly, Tinkerbell, Sonflower, Freckles, Pippi, Starbright, Kiddo, Jingles, Steverinoooooo, Bubbles, Spunky, Rosie, Kiki, Sonshine, Happy and Hubby, Cotton Candy, Dazzle, Birdie, Hallelujah Hannah, Rainbow, Tulip, Ban-Joe, Jibber Jabber, Clumsy, and Animal Quackers.

One day I sensed I was supposed to resign from the clown ministry. We had been clowning for over twelve years. I had written a letter of resignation to our pastor, but I had not turned it in yet because I was having doubts as to whether I should resign or not? Then one night we had a priest give a healing Mass at our Church. As I went forward for him to pray over me, he said, "Oh, Lesley I don't know if I can tell you this." I told him not to worry, but to just tell me what he was receiving. He then proceeded to say, "It is finished, and it is in regard to the clown ministry." I wanted to hug him but had to wait till he was finished

27: THE SONLIGHT CLOWN MINISTRY

praying over people. So afterward I went into the sacristy and told him my story about wanting to resign, and when he gave me those words, it was confirmation for me to go ahead and resign. Priests need encouragement when they say something they think God has revealed to them. So I wanted him to know he was correct in what he received from God. I knew this was "from God" and so did he, and that helped us both.

And now for some fun things from the Sonlight Clown Ministry we shared with others.... And always remember our group's theme scripture verse:

"A Cheerful Heart is good Medicine!" Proverbs 17:22

The Apostolate of Smiling:
Just a little smile on your lips:
Cheers your heart,
Keeps you in good humor,
Preserves peace in your soul,
Promotes your health,
Beautifies your face,
Induces kindly thoughts,
Inspires kindly deeds.
SMILE TO YOURSELF,
Until you notice that your constant seriousness, or even severity has vanished.
SMILE TO YOURSELF
Until you have warmed your own heart with the sunshine of your cheery countenance.
THEN...

Go out and radiate your smile!

THAT SMILE has work to do for God.

You are an apostle now, and your smile is your instrument for winning souls.

Sanctifying Grace dwelling in your soul will give a special charm to your smile, which will render it productive of much good.

SMILE ... on the lonely faces.

SMILE ... on the timid faces.

SMILE ... on the sickly faces.

SMILE ... on the fresh young faces.

SMILE ... on the wrinkled old faces.

SMILE ... on the familiar faces of your family and friends; let them all enjoy the beauty and inspiring cheer of your smiling face.

COUNT ... the number of smiles your smile has drawn from others in one day.

The number will represent how many times you have promoted contentment, JOY, satisfaction, encouragement, or confidence in the hearts of others. These good dispositions always give birth to unselfish acts and noble deeds. The influence of your smile is spreading, though you do not always see the wonders it is working.

YOUR SMILE ... can help bring new life and hope and courage into the hearts of the weary, the overburdened, the discouraged, the tempted and the despairing.

YOUR SMILE ... can help develop vocations, a priest, a Brother or a Sister.

27: THE SONLIGHT CLOWN MINISTRY

<u>YOUR SMILE</u> . . . can be the beginning of bringing someone into the Faith.

<u>YOUR SMILE</u> . . . can prepare the way for a sinner's return to God.

<u>YOUR SMILE</u> . . . can win for you a host of devoted friends. SMILE TOO AT GOD!

Smile at God in loving acceptance of whatever HE sends into your life, and you will merit to have the radiantly smiling face of Christ gaze on you with special love throughout eternity.

This was written by Rev. Bruno Hagspiel, SVD and distributed by the Marian Helpers Center Congregation of Marians, Stockbridge Mass. (Copied with permission.)

FRIENDS (July 15, 1991 LV)

Who needs 'em, you say? When they've been rough with you today. I say you do need 'em to lean on and LIFT YOU UP whenever you're blue. You see I made two to help one another and love each other too.

Friends are MY most precious gift 'cause without 'em you'll be adrift.

They'll help you get back on track toward the road of the straight 'n narrow. That's the way to ME, you see. I am a friend to you; just look around, you'll see 'n even your enemies your friends they'll be. If you forgive 'em 'n pray for 'em . . . you'll see it'll GLORIFY ME. So lean on each other and help one 'nother. You can't do it alone; "NO, NOT ME," you say in a HUFF. COME TO ME I pray, and I'll give you enough. Friends smooth out the bumps on the road of life. They lift up the valleys and bring down the mountains. Help make the way straight, you ask... friends were given to you to help you.

So accept them please, I ask of you. They aren't there to take up space and do no more; they're there to help you in whatever you do. I LOVE YOU.

28

THE MEETING OF A HOLY CARMELITE PRIEST

One night in 1996 the same young fellow discerning the priesthood, the one in our prayer group, made me aware of a Spiritual Warfare Conference in Omaha, Nebraska. He invited me to attend. I decided I would go, and before leaving for the conference, I prayed and asked God to please teach me to learn more about the Blessed Virgin Mary.

The conference was held in a hotel in a large meeting room with an aisle down the middle. The very first night I walked down the aisle I saw a priest with a brown habit on. I leaned over and asked him, "Are you a Franciscan?" He replied, "No, I am a Carmelite." I mumbled something stupid like "close enough!" Then I chickened out and kept walking.

I knew in my heart I was supposed to meet him again, but I decided to pray and ask God, "If You want me to meet this priest, then You make it happen. I will not approach him again." On the third night of praying this prayer, I did not know where he was and was not even looking for him or thinking about him. I got up from my seat, and when I got to the center of the aisle, there he was, right in front of me, and we were face to face! Of course, I knew what I had been praying for, so I knew this was a "meeting made in Heaven" and God wanted me to meet him.

So I asked him if he would pray for me. He said, "YES!" and off we went to a little room they had set up for prayer. We were alone, and he prayed over me and blessed me with a relic of the TRUE CROSS and a relic of St. Therese of Lisieux. Remember he was a Carmelite priest! WOW, what a special blessing.

Then he asked me if I would pray over him. I had never prayed over a priest before; he was my very first. My heart was pounding out of my chest, and I thought he must have heard it as I replied, "Sure!" And so I did. This was the beginning of a long friendship as we exchanged addresses and phone numbers, and the next morning we waved to one another from across the room as the retreat was over. His name was Father Richard of the Mother of God, OCD. Remember my prayer to get to know the Blessed Virgin Mary? Well God answered my prayer by leading me to Fr. Richard OF THE MOTHER OF GOD, OCD!

I was really "flying high" and felt like I could fly home without the airplane. On the flight I kept "getting words" to write to him. But I did not have anything to write on. So what did I do? I ripped open a barf bag and wrote my first letter to my newly found priest. Of course, after I arrived home, I typed those words and mailed my first letter to

28: THE MEETING OF A HOLY CARMELITE PRIEST

him. Then the waiting began. One week went by and no letter, then two, then three weeks, and still no word. I went to the mailbox every day, and on the final day I found the mailbox empty, I looked up to God and prayed, "I thought you wanted me to meet him for some reason, but I guess I was wrong. I will pray for him as long as I live and beyond. I give him back to YOU GOD!" Then, as I opened the door to go into the house, the phone rang. YEP, you guessed it.... It was the very same priest! God had answered my prayer, and as soon as I gave the priest back to GOD, He gave the priest back to me! God is good all the time, all the time God is good.

And so began a long-distance friendship with letters back and forth and phone calls. Then one day he asked me to pray for something for him. He told me that a Madré in Mexico, who had started a new Order of Sisters in 1992, The Trinitarians of Mary founded by Madré Lillie, had asked him to be their spiritual assistant and their pastor. He wanted me to pray to ask God if he should accept this or not. I then asked him, "What is their main purpose?" He replied, "They pray for priests!" WOW! THEN I knew why God had placed us on each other's paths. I told him he needed to ask others to pray for his discernment too because I already knew he was supposed to go. And after he had received permission from his Carmelite Order, he was allowed to go to Tecaté, Mexico to be their spiritual assistant and pastor for the Trinitarians of Mary. (They are currently serving in two places in Mexico and two in the USA.)

Father Richard would come across the border and call me on a pay phone as cars whizzed by. He usually called me once a month in addition to our monthly letters to one another. One day after he had been there for a while, he called and said, "You need to come to Tecaté to meet Madré Lillie and give your testimony to the Sisters."

So in 1998 I flew to San Diego where he and a couple of Sisters picked me up at the airport. I was so embarrassed as when he went to pick up my very large suitcase that was so heavy, he almost fell onto the carousel. I guess I didn't know about packing lightly at the time!

He had warned me ahead of time they did not have hot water or electricity. I was relieved to learn they had both, although water was in short supply. Once I took a shower and they ran out of water. One Sister brought me some cold water in a pail I was able to use to get the soap out of my hair.

The day I arrived, Madré Lillie (founder of the Trinitarians of Mary) was having surgery. We were on our way to visit her. As we approached the street to cross, all the traffic came to a full stop in both directions. They respected religious nuns and priests, and they allowed us all to pass across the street. If you know the history of Mexico, this was a great change in how they treated priests and nuns back in the 1920s.

I was in the waiting room of the clinic with Father and a Sister. There was also a Seminarian from Mexico who was going to be entering the Seminary in the USA. He asked me to pray for him. He is now a priest in California. Praise God!

28: THE MEETING OF A HOLY CARMELITE PRIEST

Father Richard and I were able to visit Madré after her surgery. And when it was time to take her home one of the Sisters drove the car. Madré sat in the front seat and the priest and I sat in the back seat. They had to stop to get her prescriptions filled, and I was left in the car alone with this beautiful Madré. I sat right behind her, and she had a severe headache. I was holding her head between my hands, and I felt like I was holding the head of a future Saint! It was a beautiful experience for me.

When we arrived at the Monastery, the Sisters were gathered behind the closed doors of one of the chapels. Then the doors opened, and God's beautiful Sisters all sang the Salve Regina. It was beautiful. They all said, "Bienvenida!" and I made a fool of myself by replying "Bienvenida" back to them! I learned later they were saying "WELCOME!" to me! They must have had a good laugh at my reply!

Another funny thing happened while I was there. We had a candlelight procession that ended in the Church. One of the Sisters asked me to hold her candle, as she was the cook that day and had to go to start dinner. The candles had paper wrapped around the bottom so the wax would not drip onto the floor. So as I was holding her candle and my candle, I was praying and had my eyes closed. One candle tipped toward the other one and set the paper on fire. I was stomping the fire out on the concrete floor. But it re-lit, so I then ran up the center aisle with my "on fire" candle! I caused quite a scene, and I am sure the poor Sisters had to stifle their laughter once again at this crazy "gringa!"

The first time I traveled to Tecaté it was the middle of summer, and it was HOT. The sweat poured down the center of my back like a river. The poor Sisters had their habits on, so I can only imagine how hot they must have been. Sacrifice to the max!

I was able to give my testimony to the Sisters, but the Madré was sick the whole time I was there. She asked me to pray over her, and so I did. I had never prayed over a nun before. I held a third-class relic of Padre Pio to her head. It was a piece of his habit a friend had given to me given to her by a priest who knew him well. He is now Saint Pio of Pietrelcina.

One day Father and I had lunch at an outdoor restaurant. I looked up, and a man in a military uniform held an AK 47. It was quite a scary moment for me as I was not expecting that! I was fortunate as nothing bad happened while I was in Mexico the first time, and thanks be to God I returned safely home.

After two more years, in 2000, one day Father Richard of the Mother of God, OCD telephoned me and told me I "needed to come to Tecaté again and share my story with Madré Lillie" as I was not able to do so the first time.

So off to San Diego I flew again, where the priest and Sisters picked me up. This time I took a much lighter suitcase. Then we drove on to Tecaté.

The second time in Mexico I was able to meet again with Madré. We were in the sacristy, before Mass started. I shared my testimony of how God wants me to build a priest's retreat on the fifteen acres called the "Top Lot."

28: THE MEETING OF A HOLY CARMELITE PRIEST

She listened to my story, and I finished by asking her if she might be able to help us. She smiled and replied very softly, "Yes!"

I replied "YES?"

And she said, "Yes," again!

After we both said "YES" a few times, we both laughed. She told me she would give us five Sisters to help on the "Top Lot" once it is "up and running." Then she said, "Let's ask Father Richard to come into the sacristy so I can ask him if he is willing to help too." He then entered the sacristy, and she said to him, "We are going to help Lesley!"

He asked her, "How long will we be able to help her?"

Madré then took my hand and his hand, and he took my hand, so the three of us were united. THEN she replied, "We will help her forever and ever till death do us part and throughout all eternity!"

WOW!!! I almost passed out with JOY! What a beautiful blessing! I felt I was in the presence of two future Saints.

While at the Monastery, we had a nighttime procession with all of the Sisters. As Fr. Richard and I walked along, we had to keep lighting each other's candles as it was a windy night, and they kept blowing out. That had great meaning to me, that we were meant to help each other to keep going and to never give up with what God led us to do. AMEN!

One time we, Fr. Richard and I, walked up the hill in the daytime to the large cross at the top of the mountain. Father and I were talking, and I had told him about my husband's grand uncle, Fr. John Anthony Fox M.S., being a priest. He had passed to eternal life in 1939 while carrying the Blessed Sacrament in London, England. Then Father Richard told me that "whenever you have a priest in the family, he will always pray for you, and that is probably why you have a love for the priesthood and why you became a Catholic." Who knew? Not me!

Another time Father and I walked up the mountain and we talked again about God's calling on my life, that of praying for priests and building a retreat center for them on the "Top Lot." And he said, "Lesley, a priest takes many with him wherever he goes, whether it be to Heaven or to Hell." That comment was like a sword going through my heart and was even more of a confirmation for the "Top Lot." If you think about it, it makes a lot of sense. So many people leave the Church because of a priest not being holy. And a Holy priest helps many to Heaven.

When I was in Tecaté, one day I walked up the hill by myself to the huge Cross at the top. I sat on one of the chairs and suddenly my "fanny was on fire!" I had sat where there were red ants! So I practically ran down the hill and told one of the Sisters. She brought me to the first-aid area where we promptly put hydrogen peroxide and calamine lotion on my fanny. This helped to relieve my pain a bit.

Those poor nuns must have had such a laugh over the things that happened to me as I visited them.

One time Father Richard visited us in Florida. My husband was still working and left for work at 8 a.m. Father

28: THE MEETING OF A HOLY CARMELITE PRIEST

would not be alone with me in the house, so each day we would get in my car and drive to different Catholic Churches. As an Order (Carmelite) priest, they are taught to never be alone with a woman. He took his vows very seriously. Praise God!

My dear holy priest passed to eternal life on July 14, 2014. He had had a life of suffering since the age of twenty-six. He had cancer of the eye and had his eye removed followed by radiation to the side of his face. The radiation affected his speech, and he had a loss of hearing in the ear on the same side of his face. This made it very difficult for others to understand him until they got used to his speech. He wore a covering over his eye for the rest of his life. He had cancer several times over the years and finally succumbed to brain cancer after many years of suffering. Eternal rest grant unto him O Lord, may Your perpetual light shine upon him, may he rest in peace. Amen.

I have confidence he is praying from Heaven for us and for all of God's priest sons. I always ask him to pray to God for specific priests.

Fr. Richard of the Mother of God, OCD was a faithful priest who spent much time over several years helping me. I miss him every day, but because of the communion of Saints, I know he is still helping us from Heaven. I pray for him to help me get to Heaven one day where we can rejoice together and pray for God's priest sons still down here on earth. Praise God.

29

A MEETING WITH THE BISHOP

My husband and I met with our Bishop in NYS in 2019. As we spoke with him, he sat on a small sofa and my husband and I sat on two chairs. My husband gave him a little of our working history. As I shared my testimony with him, he mentioned just that very morning he had had a meeting with some of his priests. They discussed how they could help the priests of the Diocese. WOW! Another GODcidence!

There are five areas he wanted to help the priests of his diocese: 1) spirituality, 2) communications with young and old, 3) theology, 4) liturgy, and 5) management/delegating. He felt the "mission" of the "Top Lot" would fit in with "growth in spirituality." Praise God!

He was very interested in my testimony. He said "it would be good to have hermitages." When he said this, my eyes started to tear up a bit because that is exactly what I had "received" so many years before. We are supposed to

29: A MEETING WITH THE BISHOP

have a single hermitage for each priest. When he said this, I asked him, "Can I come and sit beside you?"

I am sure he was surprised, but he said "YES!"

THEN, I asked him for a hug, which he gave me. He also told us he would not interfere with our project. He liked it when lay people came up with inspired plans. The Diocese did not have any money to offer, but the prayers of a bishop are even better than money. We will have to pay for this project ourselves, but I know in my heart GOD WILL PROVIDE.

After I shared my conversion story with him, he said to me, "You have been a Catholic since you were a baby!" All glory be to God!

As we left, he looked at me and said, "Thank you for coming!" He then said "Not many would come to meet a bishop and share their story. You have a lot of courage and faith."

I replied, "I knew this was 'from God,' so it was not hard for me to do, and I was not afraid."

Then he said, "Thank you, both of you, you made my day!"

I replied "We made your day? Well, you really made my day!" I have been waiting years for this day! Then I asked him to give us a blessing as we prepared to leave. He put his arms around both of us and prayed the Saint Francis blessing over us. (Numbers 6:24-25)

All the way home, an hour drive, I kept saying/yelling "HALLEJUIAH" at the top of my lungs! I am sure hubby was thrilled about that!

30

PRAYING FOR OUR PRIESTS

> "Come to Me, all you who labor and are burdened, and I will give you rest."
> —Matthew 11:28

Praying for our priests is so very important. Praying from our hearts is a great way to pray; let the Holy Spirit lead your prayer. I also have two little books I use to pray for them every day. One is *Praying for Our priests in Purgatory* (Shalom Publishers), and the other is *Praying for Our priests* by Monsignor Peter Dunne and Vicki Herout by Maria Regina Cleri.

Another GODcidence occurred in regard to this booklet. I was at a local Catholic Church, and they had a library. I signed out this booklet. I came home and sat in a chair and praying from the book down by our lake. All of a sudden, the book flipped out of my hands and into the lake! Of

30: PRAYING FOR OUR PRIESTS

course, I could not return it as the pages were all ruined. I contacted Vicki Herout, and she sent me several booklets. Over the years I have ordered many more of these, and I have handed them out to many people and encouraged them to also begin praying for priests. God took something bad, the book jumping into the lake, and turned it to something good!

Another good booklet to pray from is the *Chalice of Strength Prayers for priests* by Crusade for priests (Opus Sanctorum Algelorum 164 Apollo Road SE, Carrollton, OH. 44).

I have been waiting patiently and sometimes not so patiently since March 30, 1991 for this "mission" to come into fruition. We have met with two bishops, and they have both approved the plan but offered no monetary support.

Now that my forever husband and I are both retired, we were able to build a home up on the "Top Lot" as a new beginning and our future place of operations. Then in 2022 we formed a corporation in Florida as the first step in setting up for a non-profit 501-C-3. We have had several people give us donations over the years, so we had earmarked that money, and recently we opened a "Top Lot Ministry for Priests" bank account.

Currently we are waiting for the nonprofit to be approved; we applied over a year ago and are still waiting. Please help us with your prayers for this to move forward. We will begin by building one hermitage and continue as the money comes from those who will support us in this endeavor.

Things are beginning to move forward now. Over the years, after sharing my story with others, several had told me "YOU NEED TO WRITE A BOOK!" I have made four attempts at writing before, but this time I succeeded. Thanks be to God!

One gentleman, I had recently met, after hearing my testimony told me "You need to write a book!" Then he gave me a $1,000 check. THEN within a week, I received another check for the same amount, this time from a Franciscan priest who knew me well. He did not know the other person, and he did not know he had given me a check. He also said, "YOU NEED TO WRITE A BOOK." Then another Franciscan priest told me the same thing within a few more weeks. These three did not know one another, and within a few weeks' time, things began to move forward. So I took this as a confirmation now is the time!

With the prayers of Saint Pio of Pietrelcina praying for the "Top Lot" and for us, I know it will happen soon. Other Saints interceding for us are St. Francis of Assisi, Saint Maximilian Kolbe, Saint John Vianney (Patron Saint of Parish priests), and many other Saints, the Souls of priests in Purgatory and those already in Heaven. Blessed Solanus Casey OFM Capuchin used to say, "THANK GOD AHEAD OF TIME!!" And so let's all do that!

Now I come with my begging bowl out, like St. Francis of Assisi, every day I pray for all the priests here on Earth and those in Purgatory and I ask those priests in Heaven to pray for us to fulfill God's work here on Earth. I look forward to meeting them someday where we can all rejoice

30: PRAYING FOR OUR PRIESTS

together, and we can pray for our priests still here on earth. I ask them, and you, to pray for this mission God has placed upon my heart. We must also pray for vocations to the priesthood.

So this "little donkey" is once again reaching for the carrot. I know God gave me this "mission" for His priests, but I also think He gave them to me to help me get to Heaven. One day I drew two birds: one was above the other, the bird up above represented the priest, and his prayers covered the bird below him, me. The prayers of the bird under the priest helped the priest lift up to keep him flying.

Of course, I pray specifically for those priests who have been placed upon my path here on Earth. I will not mention all of them, but I know they pray for His "Grand Plan" too. And I thank God for them every day and give thanks to God for them. I pray for them to be HOLY priests, to be FAITHFUL to God, and to be Saints in Heaven one day. That prayer was a beautiful prayer given to me by another dear priest, one of "God's precious priest sons!" AMEN. To GOD be all the glory!

I beg you all to please pray for our priests; they all need our prayers to "keep them flying." I also give thanks to God daily for all the laypeople, priests, and nuns who support this mission with their prayers, with their encouragement and donations. God is good all the time, all the time God is good! AMEN!

31

"YOU ARE THE GOD MOTHER OF ALL PRIESTS."

This comment was said to me one day by a priest. I took it to heart and was very "touched" by his statement. I pray to God HE does use me to help all priests, either with my prayers or by us giving them a place to "lay their weary heads!" To God be all the glory!

Encourage your priests. Priests are human too, and they need much prayer. To those who have been given much, much will be expected of them. Priests have been given so much, and this is why we must pray for them. It is not easy being a priest. Can you imagine listening to everyone's confessions and knowing you have committed some of the same sins? Of course, they go to confession themselves. They have so many types of personalities to deal with. Some people are angry, some kind and gentle. So many different issues they must help solve. Remember they are human too and need much prayer.

31: "YOU ARE THE GOD MOTHER OF ALL PRIESTS."

And of course, the priest scandals also affected our good and holy priests. We cannot deny there are some priests who failed God in their priesthood. They abused children and caused our good and holy priests to be affected also.

These priests who have fallen have placed the nails in the hands and feet of Jesus on the Cross. Lord have mercy!

It must be so difficult for our dear good and holy priests to know others do not trust them because of the sins of their brother priests.

We must also pray for healing for those children who were abused by priests. And we need to pray for those who abused them too. I am sure that will be a difficult thing for some of us to do. Lord have mercy.

The Top Lot will be a place for our good and holy priests "on the front lines of battle" to have a place to rest their weary heads for a day, a week, or a month.

"Come to Me, all you who labor and are burdened, and I will give you rest."

—Matthew 11:28

32

EXPERIENCES WITH DIFFERENT PRIESTS OVER THE YEARS

One night after Mass, a very elderly visiting priest sat in the last pew of our Church. Many people went up to speak with him after Mass. I waited, and waited, and waited, because I "felt led" to go up to him, and so I waited.

When I was finally able to speak with him, he shared with me he looked forward to meeting his mother in Heaven. She had died during his childbirth, and he had never gotten to meet her.

I just happened to have a pamphlet about the "Top Lot Ministry for Priests" with me. As I shared the story of the "Top Lot" with this visiting priest, he began to get more and more excited as he saw the photos. For some reason I felt led to ask him what Order he was with. He shared he belonged to La Salette Order of priests. Lo and behold, my husband's great uncle was also a La Salette priest, Fr. John

32: EXPERIENCES WITH DIFFERENT PRIESTS

Anthony Fox MS (may he rest in peace). This elderly priest knew his brother, who was also a priest, and he knew their family in Connecticut. Small World! Another GOD<u>cidence</u>! God is good all the time, all the time God is good.

My husband's great uncle, Fr. John Anthony Fox MS, died of a heart attack while carrying the Blessed Sacrament on Holy Thursday in London, England in 1939. Old family letters reveal thankfulness he did not have to endure World War II. May he be resting in peace. I ask him to pray for us daily.

Another time, after Mass in Florida, there was a priest from Steubenville, Ohio who concelebrated the Mass. As he processed down the aisle, he came right up to me as I sat at the back of the Church. He then said, "Do you know what contemplative prayer is?"

I said, "Yes, I have just been learning about it."

Then he said, "You have just been given the gift of contemplative prayer!"

WOW! His name was Fr. Luke, and he certainly gave me much hope. Priests have no idea of how they affect others in such a beautiful way by just sharing a few words they have received from God.

Another dear priest from Colombia, Fr. Jorge, told me one day "if you believe that God has given you this mission, then you must also believe that HE will do it!" AMEN! Another beautiful story about him is when my daughter was pregnant with her first baby. She was due the same month as his birthday. He said, "The baby will be born on my birthday!"

She went into labor on his birthday, but labor was not progressing. The doctor decided she needed to have a Cesarean section. It was 11:45 p.m. on the night of this priest's birthday. I asked the doctor if the baby would be born before midnight? He said, "YES!" and she was born on this priest's birthday. When she was six months old, my daughter and I took him to a Colombian restaurant to celebrate. It was so precious to see him hold her, knowing they had the same birthday. He is another priest that encouraged me so much.

Once we had a priest stay with us in Florida for five weeks. He was a retired chaplain of the NY Yankees. He shared a saying with me once when he was a little impatient about waiting for a traffic light to change. He said, "Patience is a virtue, possess it IF you can; it is seldom in a woman and NEVER in a man!"

He gave a retreat for a nearby Catholic Church while he was with us. I went as a clown and handed out scripture verses supporting his talks.

A year later something beautiful happened with this same priest. He was the priest working on a cruise ship, and he had a stroke while out at sea. He was in a hospital in Trinidad/Tobago. I just so happened to be on the phone with a dear friend from there when I heard about him. She had a close friend still living in Trinidad. She called her friend, and she was able to visit Father in the hospital while he waited for a priest from his Order in the USA to fly down to take him home. Another "GODcidence!

Another priest who stayed in our home for three days was Fr. Stan. He attended a rally our Church gave at a

32: EXPERIENCES WITH DIFFERENT PRIESTS

local college. He writes songs and poetry and travels all over the world singing his songs. I drove him to the airport at 5 a.m., and as we opened the trunk of the car to get his luggage, there was a tree full of singing birds. I told him they were singing for him, a going away gift for our Franciscan priest.

http://www.francescoproductios.com/

33

MORE GODCIDENCES

As lay people we also have no idea what we say or do each day that can bring healing or hurt to others. So be sure to be kind, loving, and gentle with all those you meet each day. Live your life in LOVE and JOY. So live your life to the fullest and give God thanks every day and every moment of the day. Because we never know what moment He will call us home. Always remember the PRESENT MOMENT IS THE ONLY MOMENT WE CAN BE SURE OF!

I drove alone one day and kept hearing words in my heart, and I started to sing them. And believe me, no one wants to hear me sing!

Those words were "O' we're one day closer to Heaven above, one day closer to the One that we love. O' we're one day closer to Lord of Lords, one day closer to our God. O' we're one day closer to the King of Kings, one day closer to the One that we love, one day closer to our God up above, one day closer to our Lord." Someday I will ask someone to set it to music!

33: MORE GODCIDENCES

Fr. Richard of the Mother of God, OCD, my dear priest, who spent much time over several years helping me, had the most influence on my life. I treasured his letters and phone calls and how much he helped me come closer to God and to Our Blessed Virgin Mary. And I pray for him to be rejoicing in Heaven. And I know he is still my greatest intercessor. He never was able to come visit us up on the Top Lot. But I am sure he is watching over it and us from Heaven above. He gave me two St. Benedict crosses, and I always keep one very close to me.

A dear Franciscan priest gave me many priests' vestments, a tabernacle, and more importantly, several relics of different Saints. Also, a beautiful chalice and paten from Jerusalem for celebrating the Mass. The fact he believes in this mission, given to me by God, means more to me than the beautiful things he has given me. A Deacon also gave me vestments. Praise God!

34

A PRIEST FROM NIGERIA AND HIS FIRST NIGHT IN AMERICA AND OTHER EXPERIENCES WITH NIGERIAN PRIESTS

One night as I was going to Mass, I walked past a priest sitting outside of the office entrance. He seemed to be waiting for someone.

After Mass he still sat there. So I went up to him and asked him if I could help him. He replied he was waiting for another priest, and he had arrived from Nigeria a day earlier than he had originally planned. I knew it was that priest's day off, so I told him, "If he doesn't show up, you can call me, and I will return and pick you up and take you to my home." Then I left for home. After about a half an hour, I received a phone call from him, asking me to come and pick him up.

34: A PRIEST FROM NIGERIA

Our son had taken our car, so I had to call a friend to come and get me and help me retrieve this priest. When we got in her, car I sat in the back seat. She stepped on the gas, and the back seat went flying backward! It was broken, but thankfully I wasn't!

Anyway, we finally arrived at my home. He had just arrived from Nigeria and was very tired. I asked him if he wanted to take a shower and change his clothes. He said, "YES!" So I showed him the bathroom, and he started to take his shower.

I went to the kitchen and started broiling a steak in the oven. Well, being the great cook that I am (NOT!) the smoke alarm went off. I ran out to the garage and flipped the switch to turn off the power to the alarm. I did not realize it also turned off the lights in the bathroom where the priest was taking his shower. My husband was still at work, so he was alone in the house with me. Can you imagine what he must have thought when the lights went out as he was showering? I also had new white towels and had not washed them yet. So when he was able to finish showering, after I had turned the lights back on, he dried himself off with my new towels. Little did I know he would be covered in little white tufts from the towel. Guess that story is good for my growth in humility. I live and I learn!

He later told me he had heard that some white people in America were prejudiced against black people. Because of this he was a bit fearful of white Americans! After what happened to him in the shower, we had a good laugh that night. And because it was so late, he slept in our home overnight. He was our very first priest that stayed in our home overnight. I took him to meet up with the other priest the next day.

This same priest later became a Chaplain for the US Army and was stationed in Iraq. He survived that but has since passed to eternal life, and I hope to meet him again someday. Eternal rest grant unto him O Lord, may Your perpetual light shine upon him and may he rest in peace. He is another priest now praying for us and for "Top Lot!" His name was Fr. Gerald, and he was from Okigwe Diocese, Imo State, Nigeria.

I had another funny experience with another priest from Nigeria, Fr. Elias, a Claretian Missionary priest from Nigeria; he is the head of a seminary there. He had come for lunch to our home on "Top Lot." I made grilled cheese and tomato sandwiches. I had some spreadable cheese and crackers on the table, and he and my husband talked. He asked my husband what was on the crackers. He replied, cheese! I was just getting ready to put the cheese on the grilled cheese and tomato sandwiches, when he said, "I am allergic to cheese!"

YIKES!! What to do? Hubby saved the day when he said, "How about if we use steak and tomato?"

The priest said, "Great!"

We had had a steak the night before, so he jumped up and cut up some steak. So, hubby saved the day! YAY!

I learned from these experiences it is always best to ask a priest if he has any allergies or stomach issues whenever you are cooking for a priest. They are trained to eat

34: A PRIEST FROM NIGERIA

whatever is put before them. However, the last thing I ever want to do it make a priest sick. I live and I learn! Good for my growth in humility!

Many Nigerian priests are very JOYFUL! We always laugh a lot whenever a Nigerian priest visits us. Another Nigerian priest had just finished praying with our intercessory prayer group in Florida. Our group had prayed all night, and in the morning the priest and I walked outside behind the Church, and there was a BIG black dog tied to a tree with a rope, but we suddenly realized he was untied. He barked and lunged toward us. The priest feared dogs. I prayed a quick prayer to St. Francis of Assisi for the dog and the priest to both be calm. The dog stopped and started to wag his tail. I went up to him and re-tied him to the tree. St. Francis heard my prayer and answered it peacefully. Praise God!

Our daughter was married by a Nigerian priest. They had their wedding reception on a yacht. His friend, also a Nigerian priest, concelebrated the Mass with him. They both came to the reception. I looked over at them on the yacht, and their eyes were huge, and they looked very uncomfortable. I found out later they did not like being on the water. But they were kind enough to come to the reception on the yacht. The life of a priest is one of sacrifice.

Another funny thing happened to me one night as I served another Nigerian priest at Mass. When it came time during Mass to take the towel, bowl, and water over for him to cleanse his hands, I had the water and the towel but no bowl! He made a funny face, and his eyes bugged out, but only I could see him. Serving priests is God's way of helping me to grow in humility.

Another Nigerian priest, Fr. Elias, who visited the Top Lot last year, was our "tour guide" this year at the Rosa Mystica retreat center in New York State for one whole day. He walked us all over to the retreat center and showed us so many beautiful things. One was a room that had over one hundred relics. It was such a blessing to be there. There was Adoration, reciting of the Rosary, followed by Mass celebrated by him. He anointed me and later prayed over both of us together. The day was a Heavenly experience.

Our dear local priest from India is also full of JOY! He celebrates Mass at two Churches in the area. He does such a wonderful job of uniting his parishioners. And he is always available to answer any questions. He is a great blessing to us all.

Another priest celebrates Mass at four Churches and drives seventy-five miles every Sunday.

We all need to pray for vocations to the priesthood!

35

MY MISSION IN LIFE THE "TOP LOT" MINISTRY FOR PRIESTS

Under The Prayer Support of Saint Pio of Pietrelcina
Our Mission Statement . . .
(5/20/01 2:45 a.m. LV)

"The Top Lot is a ministry of prayer and action for God's priests to continue to be filled with the apostolic ZEAL of the Holy Spirit for the salvation of souls."

The Top Lot Ministry for priests will be for those priests who are "on the front lines" of battle. Those who need a place to go to rest their weary heads for a few hours, days, or weeks. For our good and holy priests that need a place where they can come and "JUST BE!"

Some have visited to take a few hours out of their busy days. Some have come to the Top Lot for lunch or dinner, or just to spend a few hours at night to sit by our fire pit and stare up at the stars and reflect on God's beauty.

Some like to come and sit down by the lake and enjoy God's country.

We are available IF they want to talk; otherwise, they can be alone if they wish. We do not want to burden them in any way. And they know we can be trusted not to repeat anything they share with us; this is very important.

They can swim, paddle a canoe, rowboat, kayak, or fish from the shore. Or they will be able to take a walk down our "wood road" and enjoy the scenery. We also have the Stations of the Cross in our woods.

We have had several priests stay in our home in Florida also. Praise God!

With God's help, we will build hermitages for them to stay in as they enjoy God's Country. We will also build a chapel.

This is where we need the help of lay people to accomplish God's GRAND PLAN! Some priests have also contributed to the cause. We will use the proceeds of this book for the building of the priest's retreat. And we thank you for purchasing this book and know that our prayers are for you.

We give all GLORY, HONOR, and PRAISE to Our Lord and Savior, Jesus Christ, for bringing this "GRAND PLAN" into fruition.

Always remember to ask God what HIS plan is for your life!

PART II

Talks Given Over the Years

36

SAINT PIO OF PIETRELCINA, CAPUCHIN "OUR GO-TO" SAINT FOR THE TOP LOT!"

> "You must speak to Jesus, not only with your lips, but also with your heart; actually, on certain occasions, you should speak with only your heart."
> —St. Pio of Pietrelcina

The following is a talk I gave to our intercessory prayer group about the Saints, especially Blessed, now Saint, Pio of Pietrelcina (written 11/21/2001).

We all have Patron Saints and some "favorite" Saints. Well, today is a great day for me because it is my second anniversary of becoming a Secular Franciscan on November 21st, 1999. St. Francis of Assisi is "my guy!" My Confirmation name is Francis. He always kept it simple and joyful. Yet he suffered with the Stigmata at the same time and knew how to follow in the footsteps of Jesus in every way. He is an awesome Saint to turn to with your humble beggings. He was and still is a "beggar!" As Franciscans we "come with our begging bowl out" whenever we need something. He will pray for you. As Secular Franciscans we are "called" to prayer and penance. We are called to live the Gospel and to go from living the Gospel to reading the Gospel and back to living it again.

And now I would like to share with you about another Franciscan, one that is our "go-to" Saint for the priests retreat center. A Franciscan for our day and time. I am sure you have all heard of Padre Pio. He is now Saint Pio of Pietrelcina. He was a spiritual assistant of many. He never flattered himself. He always wrote, "To God alone and not to me give praise and thanksgiving. You owe nothing to me. I am but an instrument in the hands of God, capable of serving a useful purpose only when handled by the Divine Craftsman. Left to myself, I know how to do nothing except sin and sin again."

I think we can all relate to him; I know I can, especially about the sinning part. He had the God given virtue of HUMILITY! We all need to grow in the virtue of humility every day. He wrote the following words of advice. He established five rules for spiritual growth: 1) weekly confession, 2) daily communion, 3) spiritual reading, 4) meditation (time spent with our lord daily), and 5) examination of conscience every day at the end of the day.

Regarding spiritual reading, he always urged a thorough study of Scripture and suggested and lent spiritual

36: SAINT PIO OF PIETRELCINA

books from the friary library. "If the reading of holy books has the power to convert worldly men and women into spiritual persons, how very powerful must such reading be in leading spiritual men and women to greater perfection."

Other thoughts of Saint Pio, "Meditation is the key to progress in knowledge of self as well as the knowledge of God, and through it we achieve the goal of the spiritual life, which is the transformation of the soul in Christ."

He suggested themes from the Bible as Jesus' Passion, Death, Resurrection, and Ascension into Heaven to meditate upon. "Ask God," he insisted, "for the Grace to make good the mental prayer that you are about to undertake, so that you can derive the fruit that God most desires. Finally recommend yourself to the intercession of the Most Holy Virgin, as well as to all the Heavenly court, so that they may help you meditate well."

Saint Pio of Pietrelcina's advice to his spiritual children can be summed up in ten points, all of which apply to our daily lives. I shall share them with you now.

1.) "Put your trust in Christ as your personal Savior. Saint Pio often counseled his disciples to abandon themselves to Jesus "like a child into his mother's arms."
2.) "Know that you have no righteousness of your own. No one can worthily love God. We are NOTHING on our own, but everything through HIM."
   a.) "Never be pleased with yourself."

b.) "Do NOT complain about offenses perpetrated against you."

c.) "Always groan as a poor wretch before your God."

d.) "Never marvel at your weakness, but recognize yourself for what you are: blush over your inconstancy and faithlessness to God, and confide in Him, tranquilly abandoning yourself to the arms of the Heavenly Father, like a babe in the arms of his mother."

e.) "Never exult in any way in any virtues, but ascribe everything to God, and give HIM all the GLORY AND HONOR. Do everything for the love of God and His glory, without looking at the outcome of the undertaking; work is judged not by its result, but by its intention."

3.) "Remember that good works come only through Christ. Good works are produced only in union with Christ. All our actions are mixed with inclinations toward pride, vanity, self-love, and similar sins. But if our motives are God-centered and our actions consecrated to God, they are accepted and used for His glory. A Christian should not worry about what he does so long as it is done with a desire to please God."

4.) "Recognize that the devil is a real individual, bent on destroying you. BUT DO NOT FEAR him. You must not marvel if our common enemy has mustered all his strength to keep you from hearing

36: SAINT PIO OF PIETRELCINA

what I am writing to you. This is his job and it is to his profit. Despise him, therefore, and arm yourself against him with ever greater steadfastness in FAITH. Resist him strongly in faith. (Remember "submit to God and resist the devil and he will flee!) Do not let the many snares of the infernal beast terrify you. JESUS, who is always with you and who fights with you and for you, will never let you be deceived or conquered."

5.) "Always pray to God and say in every circumstance, "Thy will be done." Repeat this in affliction, in temptation, and in the trials to which Jesus will be pleased to subject you. Repeat it still when you find yourself immersed in the ocean of His love. This will be your anchor and your salvation."

6.) "Love the Cross. Suffering is a special sign of God's love. Without love for the cross, we cannot make much profit in the Christian life. As children of God, we must NOT grumble. Why worry whether it is through desert or meadow through which you pass, so long as God is always with you, and you arrive at the possession of a blessed eternity? Offer your sufferings to God as a sacrifice." Padre Pio did not urge everyone to offer himself as a victim soul; he did teach that "everyone should offer suffering, when it comes to God to be used for His good purposes. Physical and spiritual ills are the worthiest offering you can make to Him who saved you by suffering."

7.) "Offer every action up to God. Make short mental prayers, offering everything you do, no matter how trivial, to Christ."

"**NEVER WORRY.** Anxieties are a waste of time. The devil uses worry to befoul our good works because of our lack of confidence in God's goodness. Our sweet Lord is deprived of giving us many graces, solely because the door to our heart is not open to HIM in Holy CONFIDENCE! Pray, hope, and don't worry."

8.) "Aspire to the Heavenly prize. The JOY of paradise will be enough to carry us all on. Every sacrifice we make on earth will be rewarded. Heaven is total JOY, continuous JOY! We will be constantly thanking God!"

9.) "REJOICE IN THE LORD!" Despite His sufferings as a victim of Divine Love, Padre Pio was a cheerful man. "DRIVE MELANCOLY AWAY, JOY with PEACE is the sister of charity. Serve the Lord with laughter!" Padre Pio always advised living by FAITH and by LOVE. He seldom condemned anyone. He always stopped anyone who criticized others. "Leave JUSTICE in the hands of GOD!" When a woman asked him what she could do to become better, he replied, "LOVE, LOVE, LOVE!" "In spite of our sins?" she asked. He answered, "In spite of everything!"

36: SAINT PIO OF PIETRELCINA

Saint Pio always had a great love for Our Blessed Virgin Mary. Let us present ourselves to Her for Her intercession for us tonight, as today is the Presentation of the Blessed Virgin Mary.

37

THE "BUILDING" OF A PRIEST AND PERSEVERANCE

5/20/01 2:45 a.m. (LV)

FIRST IS HIS <u>FOUNDATION</u> ... a strong FAITH in Jesus ... a one-on-one personal relationship with Him. On <u>this foundation</u> the gates of Hell shall <u>not</u> prevail.

Pour the concrete on stable ground ... TRUE FAITH in God's Church ... in Her teachings.

First floor ... LOVE ... walk in His love with ALL those you meet, from the lowest beggar to the highest King.

Second floor ... TRUST ... in HIM ... the ONE who "called you" ... always TRUST in His MERCY and His LOVE.

Third floor ... Have "<u>NO FEAR</u> allow Him to LEAD & GUIDE you ... knowing He will ALWAYS "be there for you."

Fourth floor ... family and friends ... know God has placed "special people" in your path to help you to stay strong in Him. Don't be too proud to accept the "helping

37: THE "BUILDING" OF A PRIEST

hand of another." Even the "littlest lamb" can help you as you help him/her.

Fifth floor... TRADITION... stick to TRADITION.

Sixth floor... REST... take time to "rest in Him," but also to rest your body and soul. Do not let the pressures of everyday life pull you down.

Seventh floor... allow Mother Mary to come to and COMFORT you in your most difficult trials. Even when there are no trials... rely on Her intercession. She loves you dearly... allow Her to love you. DEPEND on Her! She will be one Lady that will NEVER let you down! Amen!

Eighth floor... priestly friendship, "lean on" your fellow priests... at least one. Share yourself with him.... Go to him often in confession. Confess your sins as you instruct others to do so. Avoid the "near occasion of sin," never put yourself in a "compromising position."

Ninth floor... be HEALTHY... take care of your body as well as your soul. Don't "stuff it with fat."

Tenth floor... a sense of HUMOR... allow the barbs of others to "roll off your back" like water off a duck's back. Many will complain.... Pray for them, as you pray for them you will be strengthened.

Eleventh floor... give of yourself always... allow Him to "use you up" totally... until the day you breathe your last... never give up! PERSEVERE.

BE STRONG IN HIM AND WEAK IN YOURSELF and He will raise you up on the last day.

Twelfth floor and all the way to Heaven... a skyscraper you will be... reaching into the Heavenlies for yourself and others. Allow His elevator to carry you to Heaven along with all those you "care for" as a Shepherd.

PERSEVERE (LV)

P... Prayer, strengthens us.
E... Eternity, keep your eyes on eternity.
R... Resurrection, God's promise.
S... Serve others, forget yourself.
E... Enjoy life as you serve others.
V... VICTORY is ours if we persevere.
E... Eucharist... daily if possible.
R... Righteousness, always strive for it.
E... Enemies... Forgive them.

38

"A PRIEST GOES TO HEAVEN OR A PRIEST GOES TO HELL WITH A THOUSAND PEOPLE BEHIND."

—St. John Vianney, Patron Saint of Parish priests

A similar version of this was shared with me by Fr. Richard of the Mother of God, OCD (RIP) on a hillside in Tecaté, Mexico one day, as we walked along a mountain path. He said, "Lesley, a priest takes many with him wherever he goes, whether it be to Heaven or to Hell."

When I heard these words, it was like a sword going through my heart as I knew in my heart this was a confirmation for the purpose for the ministry God has called us to accomplish.

Think about it, if a priest falls, it affects all of us, including other holy and faithful priests. Many lay people have left the Church because of "fallen priests."

Priests need our prayers. Please pray for those priests you know and those you don't know.

St. John Vianney is the Patron Saint of Parish priests. He prays for priests: "The priest continues the work of redemption on Earth.... If we really understood the priest on Earth, we would die not of fright but of love.... The priesthood is the love of the heart."

A Prayer for priests: "Lord Jesus, we your people pray to You for our priests. You have given them to us for our needs. We pray for them in their needs.... Let them see you face to face in the breaking of the Eucharistic Bread."

Here are some of my favorite prayer books for priests.

1.) *Praying for Our priests*, a guide to praying for the priesthood in Union with Mary, Queen of the Clergy. It includes meditations on the priesthood for the Mysteries of the Rosary and the Stations of the Cross. By Msgr. Peter Dunne, RIP and Vicki Herout. It can be ordered on their website: www.prayingforourpriests.org.
2.) *A Rosary for the Souls of priests suffering in Purgatory.* www.editriceshalom.it
3.) *Chalice of Strength Crusade for priests* https://opusangelorum.org

39

THE LIVES OF THE SAINTS

As a convert to Catholicism, I think one exciting thing about the Catholic Church is reading the lives of the Saints. Somehow when we are "down" about something it always gives us encouragement to pick up a good book about someone who has "traveled this path" before us. Reading the Lives of the Saints helped me in my conversion walk into the Catholic faith.

When we read about their lives it gives us new hope, especially when we read about all their shortcomings, their sufferings, and their "apparent" failures. We learn about how they continued by "keeping their eyes on Jesus." They NEVER GAVE UP; they had PERSEVERANCE in prayer and in penance. They knew what "KEEP ON KEEPING ON" meant!

They took every event in their lives, the huge events and the tiny, little, seemingly unimportant, insignificant, day-to-day happenings in their lives. They learned, by God's grace, to embrace it all. To give it all to Jesus to do as HE saw fit. They knew EVERYTHING occurring in their lives was first approved by the Lord Himself, before they received it. It was given to them for a greater purpose. We do not know the purpose in most cases, but He always knows the purpose. And the fact HE KNOWS should be enough to give us His peace as we walk through whatever He has allowed us to experience. AMEN!

I know we all have Patron Saints and some "favorite" Saints, right? My Confirmation name is Francis, after Saint Francis of Assisi. He always kept it simple and joyful! Yet he suffered with the Stigmata at the same time. He knew how to follow in the footsteps of Jesus in every way. He is an awesome Saint to turn to with your humble beggings. He was and still is a "beggar!" As Franciscans we come with our "begging bowls out" whenever we need something! He will pray for you. As Franciscans we are "called" to prayer and penance. We are called to live the Gospel and to go from living the Gospel to reading the Gospel and back to living it again.

If you are thinking about becoming a Secular Franciscan, you might like to check this website: The Secular Franciscan Order-USA (info@secularfranciscanusa.org) or call 1-800-FRANCIS.

40

SOME THINGS I HAVE "HEARD IN MY HEART"

In Tecaté, Mexico on the mountain top, under the huge cross:

"EMBRACE MY CROSS FOR MY PRECIOUS PRIEST SONS."

Other things at other times:

L is for <u>Looking</u> at ME always, keep your eyes on ME and off the circumstances;

O is for <u>Others,</u> seeing ME in others;

V is for the <u>Voice</u> you will use to proclaim <u>MY</u> word;

E is for the <u>Encouragement</u> you will give to others in <u>MY</u> name.

Encourage and LOVE one another always.

PRIESTS Reconcile us to God. Intercede for us and bring us the Holy... Eucharist daily. They help to... Sanctify us, for our salvation. They are a... Treasure sent by God. Treasure the priests God has given you, to help you to Heaven. And always remember to... Send prayers to Heaven for them daily.

Words in my heart after my conversion to the Catholic faith.

DECISIONS

What? DECISIONS:

The decision to love,

The decision to forgive,

The decision to decide to do what HE calls you to do....

Life is made up of decisions....

Do I trust God?

Do I give my life to Him? Do I let Him be in control?

DECISIONS... Do I get angry... or do I stay calm?

Do I hate... or do I love?

Do I stay sad... or do I rejoice in all things? Do I help others? Do I feed the poor? Do I share my laughter and HIS joy with others? YES... Life is a decision... A lot of decisions. Do I care? YES!

Do I love? YES!

Do I follow HIS ways? YES! Or my own? NO!

Life is a series of big and little decisions, but each decision affects another's life in some small way... or maybe some BIG way! Do I decide to talk about God's love to others?

Do I share myself with others?

Do I share HIM with others?

Decide TODAY... you never know how many more decisions God will give you to decide. Make the RIGHT ones... DECIDE TO NOW!!!

June 1, 1991, 12:30 a.m. (LV)

41

FAITH AND ENDURANCE A TALK FOR THE YOUTH OF OUR CHURCH

When asked to give a talk for the youth retreat, I was a bit surprised I would be asked as I thought "who would want an old lady to give a youth retreat talk?" As I was shown a list of topics, "FAITH & ENDURANCE" jumped off the page at me. Of course, I have come to realize over the years whenever someone gives a talk, it is a talk the person giving the talk needs to hear more than those receiving it. It is more blessed to give than to receive. God is usually preparing us for something, and giving a talk helps me more than it does you.

I have been trying to remember what it was like when I was eighteen. WOW, I must reach waaaaaaaaay back in my memory bank, which is a dollar short most of the time. Sometimes I think I am going bankrupt!

Anyway, I remember being a senior in high school and due to graduate soon. I woke up one night with these words on my mind.... "GENERATION AFTER GENERATION, THE DESTINY OF THIS GREAT NATION IS NOW IN OUR HANDS." Well, I didn't know God back then, at least not very well, but HE certainly knew me, just as HE knows every one of you. He knew you before you were born. He also had and does have a PLAN for your lives.

The next thing I knew they had put that statement under my picture in the yearbook. Then the valedictorian of the class used this quote in her graduation speech. My brother sat in the front row, and I could see him laughing when she read it. He had teased me about those words before.... Brothers love to tease their sisters!

Of course, the "destiny of this great nation" is really in GOD's hands, but He uses US, doesn't HE? So in a sense, the statement is true; it is up to US to say "YES" to the plan HE has for our lives, isn't it? We can always say "NO" to God's "calling" upon our lives, can't we? God is a Gentleman; He never forces us to do anything against our own will. FREE WILL. That means we have the free will to make our own decisions, the decision to do what we want, but if it is not in agreement with God's will, then we <u>will</u> be in trouble! And if all of us are open to God's will for our lives, then we truly CAN CHANGE THIS NATION AND THE WORLD!

I love kids because they are usually full of enthusiasm and HOPE for the future. They feel INVINCIBLE. They have the attitude "nothing is going to happen to me, I can do anything." This enthusiasm is good, but it must be channeled in the right direction.

41: FAITH AND ENDURANCE

Sometimes God's plan for our lives is not OUR plan. In fact, it usually happens this way, right? One of the ways to discern something is if it is against what we would normally want, then it is probably from HIM.

You are, or soon will be, trying to discern what you are supposed to do with your lives, right? Everybody is pressuring you to make a decision. What college will you go to? What will you be? What will you do with your life? I challenge you to ask GOD what HE wants you to do with your life. Each one of you has a vocation in life. Whether it be to the married life, single life, or life as a religious Sister, a consecrated virgin, a brother or a priest.

On this retreat, I ask you to ask God what HE wants you to do with your life. He will tell you, He will guide you, IF you just ASK HIM! Knock and the door shall be opened unto you; seek, ask, and keep asking. He wants to hear you ask HIM. Then be still and know HE IS GOD. You might say, "Oh but, I don't know how to pray." Just tell Him that, pour out your little hearts to HIM, and ask Him, and HE WILL help you. You don't have to have a degree in theology to pray. In fact, the simpler your prayer is, the more it pleases Him. He wants us to be humble, to "get on our knees" and turn to HIM. He loves simplicity and humility. These are two virtues we all need to grow in. They are virtues close to His heart.

Jesus died for each of us; now THAT is humility. And then HE gave us HIS most precious and beautiful "gift" of the priesthood, so that HE could bring us HIMSELF in HIS TRUE BODY, BLOOD, SOUL, AND DIVINITY OF

JESUS CHRIST to us daily in the Holy Mass, in the Most Holy Eucharist!

Every decision we make should be preceded by prayer. And every decision you make affects another. Perhaps some of you feel "called" to be a doctor? You might be the one who finds a cure for cancer or some other deadly disease. Or suppose you become a lawyer? Or a politician? Perhaps the president? A teacher? Nurse? Doctor, janitor, a printer, a maid, or a bus driver? Even the lowliest position is important if done with God's love. Perhaps God is planning to use you to help change the minds of others? This could change things in the nation.

Even if we are not called to something great, everything is great in God's eyes if we do HIS WILL. Suppose you are a janitor or a maid cleaning toilet bowls? IF we do it with LOVE FOR GOD, then He is happy with us. You can pray while you scrub that bowl. Just by being you, God's love can be shown to the world.

Have any of you read the life of St. Therese of Lisieux? She is the Carmelite Saint of the "little way." Everything she did, she did with God in mind, with pleasing HIM. From the most menial tasks to the greatest she did with love for God. Her way was the simple way. All of us can ask God to help us to see HIM in everything and in every situation in our lives, in everyone we meet and in everything happening to us.

The thing helping me so much in my own spiritual growth was reading the *Lives of the Saints*. We see how human they were, how they made many mistakes, but they "gave themselves to the Lord" and HE changed them.

41: FAITH AND ENDURANCE

We can all do BIG things in SMALL ways! OR SMALL things in BIG ways!

God calls all of us to the Vocation of Holiness, doesn't He? We are ALL CALLED TO BE HOLY!

We are all called to be Saints, not necessarily with a capital S, but at least a lower case s! Not one of us is worthy, but HE is the ONE who makes us worthy. He is the One transforming and changing us. We can't do anything on our own. Even giving ourselves to HIM is inspired by Him. The only thing we can do on our own is sin. And this brings us to FAITH! Even faith is a "gift" from God. If we think our faith is strong, it is only by God's Grace that it is strong. FAITH is what we hope for but cannot see.

Wow, this is incredible, what I call a **GOD**cidence, I just now opened my bible and wanted to try to find scripture readings on faith for this talk, and I opened it randomly and lo and behold it opened right to Hebrews with the heading PERSEVERING FAITH! Hebrews Chapter 10:19. Wow! Our God is a good God all the time! AMEN!

Let us pray HE helps us see HIM in every aspect of our lives. Do you believe that? That NOTHING happens to us without a reason? God is in control of our lives, every aspect of our lives. And nothing happens to us without it first passing through the hands and heart of Jesus. He does not cause evil in our lives, but sometimes He permits it. I know some of you are going through a very difficult time in your life. Does knowing He is in control help you? We need to "rest in Him"; we need to lean on Him. We need to sit and be still before Him. He will minister to each and every need and hurt we have. I want to share something with you helping you "carry your crosses."

YOUR CROSS by Saint Francis de Sales

The everlasting God has in HIS wisdom foreseen from all eternity the cross HE now presents to you as a gift from His inmost heart. This cross He now sends you He has considered with His all-knowing eyes, understood with His divine mind, tested with His wise justice, warmed with loving arms, and weighed with His own hands to see it be not one inch too large and not one ounce too heavy for you. He has blessed it with His Holy Name, anointed it with His grace, perfumed it with His consolation, taken one last look at you and your courage, and then sent it to you from Heaven, a special greeting from God to you, alms of the all-merciful love of God.

Remember Tears are a Language God Understands (by Gorden Jensen)

We have all been touched by tragedies lately. Joey, who we all know was hit by lightning and is in a coma. 2023 update: he has since passed to eternal life after suffering in a care center for over twenty years. May he rest in peace. Then the birth defects of little Maryssa and the pain it brought to her dear family. She survived for only a few short months. Some of us were blessed to have seen her in hospice care during her short life. Holding that precious

41: FAITH AND ENDURANCE

We can all do BIG things in SMALL ways! OR SMALL things in BIG ways!

God calls all of us to the Vocation of Holiness, doesn't He? We are ALL CALLED TO BE HOLY!

We are all called to be Saints, not necessarily with a capital S, but at least a lower case s! Not one of us is worthy, but HE is the ONE who makes us worthy. He is the One transforming and changing us. We can't do anything on our own. Even giving ourselves to HIM is inspired by Him. The only thing we can do on our own is sin. And this brings us to FAITH! Even faith is a "gift" from God. If we think our faith is strong, it is only by God's Grace that it is strong. FAITH is what we hope for but cannot see.

Wow, this is incredible, what I call a **GOD**cidence, I just now opened my bible and wanted to try to find scripture readings on faith for this talk, and I opened it randomly and lo and behold it opened right to Hebrews with the heading PERSEVERING FAITH! Hebrews Chapter 10:19. Wow! Our God is a good God all the time! AMEN!

Let us pray HE helps us see HIM in every aspect of our lives. Do you believe that? That NOTHING happens to us without a reason? God is in control of our lives, every aspect of our lives. And nothing happens to us without it first passing through the hands and heart of Jesus. He does not cause evil in our lives, but sometimes He permits it. I know some of you are going through a very difficult time in your life. Does knowing He is in control help you? We need to "rest in Him"; we need to lean on Him. We need to sit and be still before Him. He will minister to each and every need and hurt we have. I want to share something with you helping you "carry your crosses."

YOUR CROSS by Saint Francis de Sales

The everlasting God has in HIS wisdom foreseen from all eternity the cross HE now presents to you as a gift from His inmost heart. This cross He now sends you He has considered with His all-knowing eyes, understood with His divine mind, tested with His wise justice, warmed with loving arms, and weighed with His own hands to see it be not one inch too large and not one ounce too heavy for you. He has blessed it with His Holy Name, anointed it with His grace, perfumed it with His consolation, taken one last look at you and your courage, and then sent it to you from Heaven, a special greeting from God to you, alms of the all-merciful love of God.

Remember Tears are a Language God Understands (by Gorden Jensen)

We have all been touched by tragedies lately. Joey, who we all know was hit by lightning and is in a coma. 2023 update: he has since passed to eternal life after suffering in a care center for over twenty years. May he rest in peace. Then the birth defects of little Maryssa and the pain it brought to her dear family. She survived for only a few short months. Some of us were blessed to have seen her in hospice care during her short life. Holding that precious

41: FAITH AND ENDURANCE

baby in my arms and looking into her beautiful eyes was a blessing; it was like looking into the eyes of Jesus. On the drive home after visiting this little bundle of love I came to the realization I had "held the suffering Jesus in my arms." Update 2023: her older brother is now studying for the priesthood. Praise God!

For a moment we must see through the eyes of Jesus with the eyes of FAITH. HE sees the greater picture; He sees the "picture from above." We must trust and know HE knows what HE is allowing for a greater purpose. We can ask Him over and over again "WHY?" We do not know the answer to these questions. But we must TRUST in Him and know HE knows the reason. Ask Him for faith to believe HE knows what HE is allowing. We do not have the answers as to why, but someday we will be able to "know the bigger picture."

He knows what we are going through. And we are all suffering in different ways, aren't we? He feels your pain, He understands. And HE will help you. No matter what you are having trouble with, HE cares for you. He loves you. And always remember the poem "Tears are a Language God Understands."

I know it is not easy to be a true committed Christian in the world today. You will face much persecution as you stand up for HIM. Especially being a Catholic Christian, as many are under attack. Others will laugh at you, ridicule you, and scorn you. Just like they did HIM. We are all called to walk in the footsteps of Jesus, aren't we? Many just want to have the joy of Jesus but want nothing to do with His suffering. But He tells us to pick up our cross and follow Him, doesn't He?

I remember being so scared to do that when I was your age. I would rather trust in myself than to trust in Him. Who knows what He will do when we give ourselves to Him? Saying or thinking you would rather trust in yourself than God is saying you know better than He. This is a major case of PRIDE!

Now, don't get too crazy about that; we all have pride. But we must ask Him to help us be humble. It is humiliating to be persecuted by your fellow classmates for speaking up for Jesus, isn't it? It is humiliating even among your peers at this retreat. "Not me, I'm not going to give myself to Him. I want to be in control." Sound familiar. Believe me, it is familiar to some adults too.

Well, I ask you to TRUST IN HIM! I remember once not even believing there is a God. I prayed a little prayer, "Lord, if YOU are real, are you really up there, let me know, huh?" I used to be that "not me" person. But then I asked HIM to show me, to help me. You should try that if you aren't sure. He will let you know for sure!

Another thing I used to ask Him was "Lord teach me to pray." I wanted to learn how to pray. Prayer is what gets you through everything. Prayer is your strength. It helps you endure, persevere till you reach Heaven. Go to Him on this retreat with an open heart, and He will fill it up to overflowing. Prayer is nothing more than talking to God and then being still and listening to Him. It is a pouring out of your heart to Him. Simple, right?

41: FAITH AND ENDURANCE

Of course, there are many kinds of prayers. But just giving Him your heart each day and asking Him to help you through each day is a good start. Before your feet hit the ground every morning, say, "GOOD MORNING, HOLY SPIRIT!" Father Dan Doyle (God rest his soul) taught me that prayer he used to do every day when he opened his eyes, before his feet hit the floor. Prayer is what gets you through the day. Prayer is your strength. It helps you endure the rough spots of the day, to persevere till you reach Heaven. Go to him on this retreat and OPEN YOUR HEART to Him. He will fill it to overflowing. Prayer is nothing more than talking to God and then being still and listening to Him.

I remember my favorite beginner's prayer, "HEEEEEEEEEELPP!" I couldn't pray anything other than that at one time in my life. I was going through rough times, and all I could do was pray "HELP!" When we turn to HIM, He will always help. Maybe not in the way WE think He should, but He knows us better than we know ourselves. He knows how to help us and what is best for us. We don't know anything, but HE knows everything!

I am a convert to Catholicism. At one time in my life, I was very anti-Catholic. Then one day I asked God to show me the TRUTH about the Church. Did HE want me to become a Catholic? When you pray a prayer like that, you had better duck because HE will answer it! (I shared the story about the mackerel fish earlier in this book, in the chapter about my conversion, so I will not repeat it here.) After seeing this, I knew the Catholic Church was the One

JOURNEY TO THE TOP LOT

TRUE Church and I decided to enter in the RCIA program. I learned about the Eucharist, and you will remember that story earlier in this book, so I will not repeat it here.

I used to BEG God—that's right I am a beggar—to show me the TRUTH and let me know what HE wanted me to DO with my life. I wanted to know the purpose of my life. Suffice it to say God showed me the TRUTH and what HE wanted me to do with my life. (See the chapter about my conversion.)

Now you must know I did not ask Him this question at your age. I did not ask until way later. It is so beautiful you have retreats and this opportunity to know Jesus at your young age. What a blessing to know He will help you NOW; you don't have to wait till you are an old fogy, like me!

I used to pray "Please Lord, why am I here? What would You have me to DO with my life?" Please ask HIM this question while you are on this retreat. And He will help you persevere in your vocation He has called you to do. Keep begging Him, and He will reveal it to you, maybe not right away, but He will. He will also put people in your path confirming it for you.

After I entered the Catholic Church, I kept begging over and over, and one day I awoke with all sorts of things going through my mind. I started to write them all down, all these thoughts and ideas seeming to come from nowhere! The bottom line is HE wants us to build a retreat center for His priests up on the "Top Lot," a piece of property where I grew up on a farm. (Update 2023: this story is also in the chapter about my conversion.)

41: FAITH AND ENDURANCE

PERSEVERANCE IN PRAYER!!! This will help you endure. Keep begging Him to help you and HE WILL, maybe not in YOUR time, but in HIS time!

And now as I have shared this story with you about the priest's retreat and what HE wants to do with my life, I ask YOU to please PRAY for me and my husband. Pray for God to use us to provide a place for God to bring His love to His priests. When our priests have a place to rest and reconnect with God, then they will be better able to bring others to Him. The "Top Lot" will be a place where the priests on the front lines, those who are reverent and holy priests, will have a place to lay their weary heads.

I once had a very holy priest tell me a "priest takes many with him wherever he goes, whether it be to Heaven or to Hell." Think about that for a moment. What do you think is the most important moment of your life? Other than your birth of course. I feel it is your death. How we live our lives will determine where we go after we die, whether to Heaven or to Hell, with a probable "stop-over" in Purgatory.

The vocation of the priesthood is sublime in it brings Jesus to us, and it brings us to Jesus through God's priests. The most important moment of our lives is our death, and the priest prepares us for death by teaching us how to live our lives. A priest brings us Jesus in the Most Holy Eucharist daily. What vocation could be more beautiful and more awesome? Jesus is our Redeemer; He saves us to rejoice in Heaven with Him one day. He died for you and for me and for everyone else. But it is up to us to say "YES" to Him.

These words about a "priest taking many with him wherever he goes" ring in my ears as I realize my "mission in life" is to help HIS priests and His seminarians. If any of you feel "called" to the priesthood or the religious life on this retreat, please see me afterward, and we will pray together for discernment for God's will in your life. And you should meet with your priest or vocations director if you feel maybe you might be being "called."

And always remember the will of God will never lead you where the GRACE of God cannot keep you! AMEN!

To sum things up, PRAY, PRAY, then PRAY some more. As you pray, your FAITH will increase, and you will ENDURE!

And as Saint Pio used to say, "Pray, hope, and don't worry!"

AMEN and AMEN!

42

SANCTIFICATION OF THE PRESENT MOMENT 8/2/02 2:44 A.M. (LV) OR "LIVING IN THE HERE AND NOW!" NOT OUR WAY, NOT OUR WILL

When I was asked to give another talk for the youth of our Church, I began to ask God, "what would You have me speak about, Lord?" Then for the next week, each and every time I picked up a book, I kept seeing these words jump off the page at me, "THE PRESENT MOMENT!" This happened three times, then one night I awakened around 3 a.m., got up, and again opened a book and soon realized I could not concentrate, and so I began to write these words. . . .

Every moment of every day is sent to us by God. What we choose to do with these moments is entirely up to our wills. How will we respond to God's GIFT of the Present Moment? Will we protest or will we accept?

NOTHING, ABSOLUTELY NOTHING happens to us without it first passing through the hands of Jesus. His hands are big, gentle, loving, and kind. He holds us and the present moment in His hands. Remember the kids' song "He's got the Whole World in His Hands?"

Are you not part of the whole world? Are you not held by the hands of Jesus? YOU ARE! And every moment of your life, past, present, and future, is "held in the hands of Jesus." Let us take a moment to picture ourselves being cupped and protected within HIS Almighty and loving hands.

Sometimes it seems like He is squeezing us a little too tightly, right? He "puts the pressure on" sometimes! We must believe HE has a reason and a purpose for this. Thy will be done, Lord Jesus, NOT my will.

I will now share with you a secret to a happy life: ACCEPT the PRESENT MOMENT. Accept whatever is happening to you right here, right now. Learn to live in the "here and now" for in this is our sanctification. Our what? Our sanctification. In other words, our way to live a holy life, moment by moment, leading us to our salvation. Depending on how we react to each moment in our lives is important to our eternal salvation.

Sometimes we are bored by what we are doing; we constantly look ahead. As youth we are always impatient and always looking ahead. As adults we make the mistake of always looking backward. "Oh, if only I had done this or

42: SANCTIFICATION OF THE PRESENT MOMENT

that. IF ONLY this, if ONLY that." The past is the past; that is why it is called that!

Youth make the same mistake, only they look too much to the future. "If only I were smarter, if only I were older, if only I were more beautiful/handsome, if only I were out of college, if only I were married, if only I didn't have this ZIT on the end of my nose!" Remember the adage "beauty is only skin deep?" Perhaps God is showing you that you are too superficial if you get nuts about a ZIT. Remember to look deeper; beauty is in the heart, not the skin. True inner beauty is what is important to God, NOT our outer beauty.

We must learn to accept the PRESENT MOMENT! Are you stuck here listening to this old lady give this boring talk? Right here, right now? ASK GOD, what are You trying to teach me God? SURRENDER to the present moment. Remember the song "I Surrender All."

If you can't sleep at night, ask God "OK, Lord, what would You have me do, right here, right now?" Then WAIT, enjoy the present moment; do not fight it, accept it. Surrender to the present moment. Impatience is a sign of spiritual immaturity. As we grow in spirituality, we grow in accepting whatever God sends to us each moment.

Do not fight God's will. If it is HIS WILL, we suffer from something for a time, know God is in control of everything. He knows you are hurting; what are you going to learn from this hurt? Are you going to "embrace this cross" God has allowed or are you going to fight against it? Do you remember the scripture verse Matthew

16:24-26 where Jesus said to His disciples, "If anyone wants to be a follower of mine, let him renounce himself and take up his cross and follow me. For anyone who wants to save his life will lose it; but anyone who loses his life for my sake will find it." Of course, this applies to the ladies too. What would You have me learn from this experience, Lord? Whether it be a painful one or a joyful one? How are You speaking to me in this present circumstance, in this present moment? God is speaking to us always; do we listen? In all circumstances of our lives, He is speaking. Sometimes He speaks softly, sometimes not!

Ask God for an increase of faith to TRUST in Him. To know HE KNOWS what HE is doing. How are you going to respond to what HE sends you? Are you going to protest and fight? Or are you going to surrender and embrace and accept and carry your cross? GIVE IT TO HIM. LET GO AND LET GOD. SURRENDER! Knowing HE knows the reason for this trial, we don't have to know the reason yet. Read Romans 8:28 and truly believe "all things work together for good to those who love the Lord." Amen!

Without "rain in life" we would have no flowers. Bloom or grow where you are planted. Allow God's "rain" to feed you, to help you GROW. Without the "rain," without the "pain," you will not grow; you will wilt and die. Remember "no pain, no gain!" The acceptable death is "death to self" or "death to our own self will."

Now, when it rains, sometimes it pours, sometimes you feel as if you are about to drown. All the pressures,

42: SANCTIFICATION OF THE PRESENT MOMENT

all the attacks from Satan, remember who holds back the hand of Satan? God's hand! God's almighty, loving hand; accept what HE allows. He allows the rain to pour sometimes because HE knows you need to grow in trusting Him. Don't drown in your sorrows, SWIM in them until you are through the STORM. He wants you to turn to Him, to trust in Him. Accept the rain, and the SON will shine once again. Amen? AMEN!

EMBRACE the present moment ... moment by moment. Do not get ahead of God; be patient, be trusting, be believing HE knows what He is doing so you don't have to. Why are we always asking "WHY?" Then we are not accepting He knows why. Why did my boyfriend/girlfriend dump me? Why, why, why??

RELAX, remember God is in control. He sees the bigger picture from above, from eternity. He only asks you to give HIM all your "present moments" in your life. Your "every moment" give to Him. Surrender to Him; surrender your pain, your hurts, your concerns, your worries, cares, and/or concerns.

As Saint Pio of Pietrelcina would always say, "Pray, hope, and don't worry!" Give Him all your "present moments" in life; He gives them to you, now you give them back to Him.

Try this: at this present moment and the next and the next, ask God to show you to teach you what He would have you do. When you meet someone, and you are talking to that person on this retreat, ask God, "What would You have me to do or say to this person? Help me, Lord."

Surrender and accept the present moment. LISTEN for that still, small voice within you. Listen for God to guide you.

The "here and now" is the only place to be. OK, so now what? Do you see that by living in the present moment we walk with God hand in hand, side by side? We are not getting ahead of Him, we are not behind Him, but we are with Him, and He is with us. God never changes; He is the same, yesterday, today, and tomorrow. He gives us the opportunity to walk with Him, moment by moment, throughout our whole lives. In living like this, we are able to ask Him to help us when we fail, when we falter, when we are being tempted to do evil. Also living in the present moment we are able to see areas in our lives where we need to forgive others and ourselves as soon as things happen.

Sometimes the most difficult one to forgive is OURSELVES. Let us ask God for the grace to forgive others and to forgive ourselves. Forgive us Lord for not trusting in you, forgive us Lord for doing things our own way and not Your way. NOW . . . NOT Our Way, Not Our Will.

In the Lord's Prayer, He tells us to pray "forgive us our trespasses as we forgive those who trespass against us." We must forgive, this is a DECISION, it is NOT A FEELING! Oftentimes we get confused because we do not feel like forgiving. If your mom is mean and nagging, do you feel like forgiving her? But you will because HE tells us to. Take the first step and tell God you want to forgive her, you DO forgive her, and HE will do the rest. You may not feel like forgiving her. But He will give you the feeling of forgiveness sometime down the line, maybe not for a long time.

42: SANCTIFICATION OF THE PRESENT MOMENT

Remember your job is to forgive, and His job is to help you forgive. You can't forgive on your own. ONLY through Him can we forgive one another. He will help us. We must ask HIM to HELP US forgive, over and over again if need be the case.

Sometimes in life you may have someone who you were very close to and then suddenly one day this person is no longer talking to you. You may not have any idea why; you may question yourself for whatever it is you may have done to offend or hurt them, and they still may reject you. Of course, you are human, so this is going to be very painful for you. But your "job" is to forgive them and pray for them, even when you do not feel like it, remembering all along there is a reason and a purpose for everything. We don't have to know the reason, just pray. Especially in the pains in our lives, ask God, "What are You trying to teach me through this Lord?" He may reveal it to you, or He may not. Perhaps He is trying to have you realize you need to be healed of an earlier childhood rejection?

Usually when someone rejects you it is because of pain in their own lives. Someone or something has hurt them. Don't allow their pain to pull you down too, but just PRAY through the pain. Remember what I said about swimming through the rain and not allowing yourself to drown?

Perhaps God has allowed that person to hurt you because He knows you will pray for that person; maybe there is no one else who would pray for them, and God knows that you will. Because God knows you; He knows you better than you know yourself. He may allow you to be hurt for a while, knowing you will pray for that person, knowing that person needs much prayer, and thank God because HE has chosen you to help that person to Heaven. Does this make sense to you? Probably not, but it does to God! While you are going through the pain of this rejection from this person, "lift up" the pain to God and ask Him to use it to help this person who is hurting you. That way your pain will be very powerful for this other person; this is called redemptive suffering. You will be a contributing factor in that person's salvation. And that's what it's all about, isn't it? Our eternal salvation is the most important thing; that is why we were born, to glorify God and to live with Him for all eternity. And He wants to use us to help others find their salvation, and we know HE does, then we should REJOICE in everything that happens to us. In the good, the bad, and the ugly, we should Praise God in ALL things... knowing HE knows what is best for our salvation. God wants us all to become SAINTS.... Do you believe that? YOU can become a saint! How? By letting go and letting God. He will do it if you let Him! We can't do it, but HE CAN and HE WILL, if you let Him. Let us all pray for one another and for every one of us to become saints! Not necessarily with a capital S! Although some of you may be one day!

OK, so now that we see we have "all fallen short of the Glory of God," we see we have all sinned. And sin is the result of failing to TRUST in God. WE have relied on ourselves instead of on HIM. This is called PRIDE! All sin is rooted in PRIDE.

42: SANCTIFICATION OF THE PRESENT MOMENT

Now what? RUN don't walk to confession! Tell the priest your sins, and remember he is not there to judge you, but to love you into returning to God. He has heard it all before and will forget it right after you leave the confessional. The priest is God's "instrument of reconciliation," he is "in persona Christi," a Latin word meaning "in the person of Christ" (see Catechism of the Catholic Church Paragraph #1548). Do not be afraid of the priest. And if sometimes he doesn't act like Christ, remember he is very human too, and we need to pray for him. Please, please pray for our priests.

Once again, a priest once told me that "a priest takes many with him wherever he goes, whether it be to Heaven or to Hell." Think about that for a second, the way a priest is, the way he lives his life, affects many people, but a priest does not get to Heaven by himself. He needs others praying for him too. It is our duty to pray for our priests, as we help them to become more holy; we are also helping others, aren't we?

Please live in the present moment, it is in the little "day to day things," not the BIG things, but the little things, and remember that God is PRESENT in the present moment. He is present in the littlest things.... LOOK FOR HIM. Be aware of God in all things and in all circumstances. Amen!

Always remember to "BLOOM WHERE YOU ARE PLANTED!" Sometimes we may be "planted" in a home with many weeds. Maybe your family does not support your faith walk; maybe they ridicule you and criticize you and tease you. You may feel rejection by those closest to you, someone who you thought was one of your closest friends. Remember to forgive them and "bloom where you are planted."

Do not take this literally, but try to imagine yourself at the edge of a very high cliff: you are standing there, and a fierce wind is whipping at you from behind you. As you gaze out over the deep, vast hole in front of you, a hole so deep you can hardly see the bottom. I ask you now to turn around. Turn so that your back is facing that deep hole. Try to feel the wind blowing against your face. The wind is pushing you backward, backward toward a certain death. Now, I ask you to lean back and let go! Let go of your unforgiveness, let go of your pain, let go of your fears, let go of your uncertainties, let go of the past, and let go of the future; let go of the present moment. Let yourself fall backward into the ever-loving arms of GOD, into the arms of Jesus. He will catch you. You will NOT fall to your death, only to your death to SELF, your death to selfishness. Let go of your unforgiveness toward yourself. IF HE LOVES YOU THE WAY YOU ARE, WHY CAN'T YOU LOVE YOURSELF THE WAY YOU ARE AND FORGIVE YOURSELF?

By learning to live in the present moment, we are fulfilling God's word to "pray always, to pray unceasingly." We are praying our way through our lives MOMENT BY MOMENT.

And remember to bloom where you are planted, right here, right now, and remember to take time to smell the flowers! In taking time to smell the flowers, we are taking

42: SANCTIFICATION OF THE PRESENT MOMENT

time to live life moment by moment. ENJOY the present moment as it will never come to you again. Amen and amen, and may God bless you through each of your present moments!

43
"BE YEA FISHERS OF MEN" A TALK FOR THE YOUTH GROUP SUMMER RETREAT 2005

How do we fish? Are there any fishermen here? Or fisher-ladies? First you must KNOW YOUR FISH! There are many different types of fish... large and small. There are the "thinkers and the feelers." Are your fish the intellectual type? OR the sentimental type?

Second: YOU are the fishing pole. By your FAITH, people can see how you are by how you act. Are your words in agreement with your actions? Remember Saint Francis of Assisi? Preach the Gospel always, when necessary, using words. These words were attributed to him, he never actually said them, but he did live them.

Your fishing pole is your testimony, your life, YOU. Has Jesus changed your life, have you allowed HIM to touch your life? Have you allowed Jesus to CATCH YOU?

43: "BE YEA FISHERS OF MEN"

Your fishing pole must be strong enough to hold the biggest fish. Have the faith GOD will be the ONE to bring the fish in; God will be doing the fishing through you. The pole is HIS instrument. You must have the faith to believe God can and will use you to catch fish. Be humble knowing is it not you, it is JESUS doing the work. HE is using you to catch the fish for HIMSELF. Allow the fishing pole (you) to be God's instrument to "haul them in!"

How about when your faith is attacked? Are you strong in your faith? Study your faith.... Read the *Lives of the Saints*, study the Catechism of the Catholic Church.

Know your faith before you "put out into the deep!" Remember when Pope John Paul II (2023 update now Saint) told us to "put out into the deep?" You must know your Catholic faith before God can use you to go fishing. Pay attention, read, study, pray. Place the fishing pole, God's instrument, into God's hands first. Give yourself over to Jesus first; allow yourself to get "caught by Jesus." The fishing line must also be strong. The line is the Word of God, know your scriptures. Again study! Be able to say the right lines!

Next is the HOOK: it must be sharp; YOU must be sharp. This goes along with knowing your faith and your fish. You will need a big hook for some and a small hook for others. IF you use a big hook for a small person, they won't be able to swallow the hook and get caught. On the other hand, for some you must be very intellectual; you will have to quote scriptures, give theological dissertations, use a BIG HOOK! For the sentimental types, you must simply share your feelings and perhaps your own testimony with them.

Next is BAIT: NOTE to self: Bring a bucket full of "worms." Make them ahead of time... long, large worms out of different-colored hard paper in the shape of worms. Put glitter on some and label them JOY (yellow), PEACE (light blue), LOVE (red), PATIENCE (pink), KINDNESS (light green) GOODNESS (white), FAITHFULNESS (dark green), GENTLENESS (violet), and SELF CONTROL (light blue). Do these words sound familiar? Remember your Confirmation when you learned about the Fruit of the Holy Spirit? He wasn't talking about bananas or peaches!

How you are yourself is how good or bad your bait will be. Examples of bad bait or bad fruit. (Note: Bring a basket full of rotten fruit... tomatoes, black bananas, prunes, rotten apples with brown spots in them.) These represent the SIN in your life.

Others can see how rotten you are, by how you are, by how you act. Examples of bad bait are swearing, being nasty, telling dirty jokes, being negative, making fun of others, being judgmental, teasing others, gossiping behind their back, back biting your friends, being rough and crude, fighting with others, anger and having a bad temper, being obnoxious to others, being a "bully!" Showing off all the time and having a "look at me" attitude! Always thinking you are right! Bad fruit equals bad bait. Remember it is NOT about YOU, it is all about GOD!

Now if you are depressed all the time and can't help it, then go to the school counselor or your priest for help or your parents. Depression all the time may mean you

43: "BE YEA FISHERS OF MEN"

need help from a psychiatrist or psychologist. Do not be ashamed of this, be sure to ask for help.

If you are fishing with bad bait / rotten fruit, you will not catch any fish. The fish will swim away from you.

If you are like all the above rotten fruit, do not despair. That is why Jesus comes to us through the priest, as he is an instrument of God in confession. Do not be afraid to go to the Sacrament of Reconciliation. The priest is there to help you, not to judge you. He will forget your sins right after you share them with him. Be not afraid!

Youth can be a good example to the oldsters. Show up to confession; try to go at least once a month. I think the health of a community can be seen by the length of the confession line. Do your part in making our Church healthy, go to confession. Be a good example. If the rest see a long line to the confessional, maybe they will think about going themselves. BE NOT AFRAID, like Pope John Paul II said!

Be honest, gentle, patient, and kind, and listen to your fish. Take the time to listen to others, and they will jump right out of the water into your arms! People today are too busy to listen to others. By listening to your fish, you are showing you really care about them, individually. Like Jesus does, He cares about you individually, one on one. He cared enough to die on the Cross for you and for me.

So listen to your fish by "dying to self"; remember it is not about you, it is about God.

Be patient, sometimes you must return to the same fishing hole day after day after day, waiting for the fish to take the bait. When you are waiting to catch your fish, be patient and PRAY for the fish. You must be patient! Fishermen/women get up early in the morning and go to their fishing spot. PRAY as you wait for the bite.

Be still, be quiet, don't move, wait. First wait upon the Lord, then wait upon your fish to bite the bait. Before you go fishing, go to the Lord and wait upon Him in prayer. Preferably before the Blessed Sacrament, the Most Holy Eucharist.

Prayer will prepare you to be patient, loving and kind. Before you "go fishing" ask God for a BIG catch this day. Sometimes your fish will nibble a few times; wait in patience, quietly for the big bite. Then pull him/her in, don't hesitate. Invite them to Church with you. If you sense the time is right, ask them if they would like to receive Jesus into their hearts. If they say yes, lead them in a short prayer of repentance, forgiveness, and ask God to help them as they turn their lives over to Him. Pray from your heart, and let the Holy Spirit lead your prayers.

Next, after you have caught your fish, or rather Jesus has used you to catch His fish, help keep him fresh and alive. And remember to release him/her to God. Catch and release them to God. Give them up and return them to God. Always remember you are <u>not</u> in control, <u>God is</u>. You are just the fishing pole, the instrument. Let them go to Jesus. Don't become too involved in all their problems. Pray for them and let them go to God.

Remember God wants to use you again and again, so keep on fishing. You've heard the expression to keep on truckin', well now you need to keep on fishin'.

43: "BE YEA FISHERS OF MEN"

Be there for them. Invite them to youth group; help them by answering questions and praying for them. But remember do not be too attached to your fish. Release them to Jesus.

Note: next, hand out different-colored gummy worms to each kid as a reminder to be "Sweet Bait" for others!

The idea for this talk "came to me" while listening to a talk by Fr. David T. at our monthly revival on May 1st, 2005.

44

TALKS FOR THE "ARMY OF GOD" INTERCESSORY PRAYER GROUP

(Jan 11, 1995, LV)

God knows I need to review my talks and renew my own life. God is good all the time, all the time God is good! He knows I need to be revived myself and to "practice what I preach!"

As I began to write this talk, I received some words (for discernment please). The Kingdom of God is within My little ones. As you bow before ME, you should bow before one another, for I AM in each of you. I am the Living Christ, and I am within each of you; respect and love one another as I am within them and within you.

How can we criticize and cut down one another when we realize Jesus in in each one of us? If we are cutting down and not building up, we are hurting the Kingdom of God. As was mentioned last week... PRIDE is the "root of all evil" of our disunity.

44: TALKS FOR THE "ARMY OF GOD"

If we can look at each other and realize and <u>believe</u> Jesus is within us, then we should treat everyone with awe and the utmost respect.

Does Jesus shine through us? And within us? What can we do to let HIM shine more? Crush the head of pride, resentment, anger, bitterness, unforgiveness, envy, gossiping, judging others, and jealousy. Satan has sneaky ways of getting us off track, such as self-pity and all the above sins. We must continue to ask God to "Create in us pure hearts and steadfast spirits, O Lord." Psalm 51:10. We must hold every thought captive, and when we begin to criticize, STOP! We must submit to God; rebuke the Devil and he will flee. (James 4:7)

We must "moment by moment" submit to God. This is a GRACE we must ask for and pray for. Ask for the grace to be able to see Jesus in ourselves and in one another. Ask to be able to BELIEVE Jesus is in us. And if HE is in us, we must reach out and touch Him in one another when we need HIM. Sometimes our pride stops us from reaching out to one another. We must reach out with the Jesus in us. Reach out to help and to serve one another. It is more blessed to give than to receive. (Acts 20:35)

Pray for others to see the Jesus in us, and for us to see the Jesus in others. Sometimes it is very difficult to see the Jesus in ourselves and in others, but we must walk by faith in His holy word and believe what He tells us in His word. Claim it and believe it! (2 Corinthians 5:7)

Remember God always keeps His promises, and HE never makes mistakes!

Now for a little story about when some of us went out into a very poor neighborhood to deliver Christmas presents to the kids. I went as "Angelina" the angel sent by God. They all ran up to receive their gifts. My job was to tell the kids the next day was the birthday of Jesus. And God had sent me on a special mission to tell them about Jesus and why He came. One little boy backed up and his eyes were as big as saucers as he looked up in awe at me.

He stammered, "Could you do me a favor? The next time you see Jesus annnnnnn God, could you tell them that I love them very much?"

I said, "Sure, but you know what? God is always with us, and you can tell Him right now!"

The little fellow said, "But I can't see Him." (Out of the mouths of babes!)

I told him Jesus is in us and that I could see the Jesus in him, and he could see the Jesus in me. That we can't see Jesus with our eyes, but that we need to believe that He is there.

"OOOOHHHHHH," he said, then he asked me, "Where are your wings?" So precious, and I hope I meet him in Heaven one day! Praying I get there!

We must avoid stifling Jesus. Remember how Archie Bunker always "stifled" Edith? Well, we must not allow the seven deadly sins to stifle the Jesus within us. He gets hidden behind our pride, envy, etc. We must come before HIM in HUMILITY and in LOVE and ask HIM to give us HIS grace to forgive others for their trespasses. To allow us to see through HIS eyes to see each other as HE sees us. We must ask Him to see past their/our errors and human ways to instead see their Jesus ways. We must look for the good and not the bad. Pray for the good of God to shine through us onto others to help bring them to salvation as well as ourselves. Pray for God's saving love to come forth, for He calls us to love one another as HE loves us (John 13:34). Do NOT be afraid to reach out to others, to touch the Jesus in them, and don't be afraid to have them reach out to you. To the healing Jesus in you. Comfort and heal one another through the Jesus in one another (John 17:22-23).

Let us pray, "Lord Jesus, we come before you tonight with humble and contrite hearts, and we ask You to open our hearts to you once again, so that Your Holy Spirit can once again fill our hearts, our minds, our bodies, souls, and our spirits with Your Holy Spirit. Open our eyes to see the Jesus in others and in ourselves, Lord Jesus. Help us to see others as You do, to see when others need You through us. When they need Your comfort, healing, and love through us. Let our touch be Your touch, Lord Jesus, help us in our disbelief, help us to trust in Your word, Lord Jesus. In Your Holy Name We Pray. AMEN!"

45

HOW TO PREPARE FOR INTERCESSORY PRAYER OR RATHER HOW TO ALLOW HIM TO PREPARE YOU

Examine your conscience daily. Is there anyone I need to forgive? Spouse, child, workplace? Ask God to reveal to you the areas you need to "work on."

You can't be an effective intercessor if you are a "dirty instrument" as with my son's trumpet here. (Note: I brought my son's trumpet as a visual.) If you have valves sticky with sin, the sound won't be sweet. You will hit sour notes, unpleasing to our Lord. We must dismiss all worldly thoughts and allow our "instruments" to be well oiled with the Holy Spirit. Make us clean, O Lord; make us well-oiled instruments, O Lord, so we will make a sweet sound for You. Go to confession often. Ask God to create in me a pure heart and a steadfast spirit within me. (Psalms 51:10)

45: HOW TO PREPARE FOR INTERCESSORY PRAYER

We must spend quiet, quality time with the Lord, even Jesus did so with His Father. (Matthew 14:23) He did this to teach us the necessity of interior prayer with prayer and meditation. Spend time in Adoration before the Blessed Sacrament.

Be still and know that I am God, He tells us in Psalm 46:10. Let Him lead us first, only then will we be effective intercessors. Let Go and LET GOD! Healing is a continuous process. We must be healed from twenty years ago (or more) or two hours ago or maybe even two minutes ago!

Other things helping prepare for intercessory prayer are fasting, praying the Our Father, the Glory Be, the Creed, the Rosary, the Saint Michael prayer Divine Mercy chaplet, and prayers of protection to our Guardian Angels.

Call upon the angels and Saints to protect us from evil and to intercede for us. Plead the Precious Blood of Jesus to protect and cover us.

Combine our prayers with the Church militant and the Church suffering in Purgatory. And with the Church Triumphant, those in Heaven. We are NOT alone!

We must keep our eyes on Jesus and not on others, for when we keep our eyes on others, we become critical and unloving. We need to look at ourselves. He calls us to LOVE, and perfect love casts out all fear. Pray for God's perfect love.

Prepare for WAR. But remember the battle belongs to the Lord, and the final victory has already been won by our Lord and Savior, Jesus Christ.

If you are a new Catholic, you must go to a Life in the Spirit seminar before joining an intercessory prayer group.

It is strongly recommended to take a prayer and healing class. If you don't know how to swim, would you jump into deep water without a life jacket? Intercessory prayer is deep water. Satan will do all he can to drown you, so please be prepared. Don't jump in without a life jacket!

Another way to prepare yourself is through praise and worship. Know Satan hates the sound of praise, worship, and laughter. Ask God to give you a joyful heart despite all your trials and tribulations. Be joyful always. (1 Thess.5:16) The JOY of the Lord is our strength. (Nehemiah 8:10)

Intercessory prayer is a sacrifice. We are a living sacrifice for God for others, we are giving of ourselves for others, we are praying for others, not for ourselves, not for the "warm fuzzies." We are oftentimes blessed by our prayers for others, but that can't be our reason for praying. We must be willing to give of ourselves for others' lives.

46

KEEP YOUR EYES ON JESUS

Hebrews 12:2
A talk for Intercessory Prayer
6/21/1995

We always hear these words but just what do they mean? And how do we do it? God is so awesome; he deals with each one of us in a unique way because HE made us as unique individuals. No two alike. Thank God! Who could take two of me?!!

He shows us things matching our personalities. For me He often gives me symbolic "movies in my mind." Such as this one.... (Show the drawing of the Eucharist with eyes on top of it.) Now at first you might not comprehend just what HE is trying to show us. But look again, and it makes perfect sense. This is the EUCHARIST... this is JESUS... and our eyes are on Jesus. We are looking at Him! Which means we must keep our eyes on Jesus. Keep focused on Him.

So just what does that mean? It means we must not get carried away by the circumstances of life. We must dwell on JESUS, not on the circumstances.

Many times, we dwell on the problems in our lives, or the daily irritations, our jobs, our spouses, our neighbors, our kids, or our houses. Or we might have a family member with an incurable disease or someone in chronic continuous pain. Or we might be caught up in a situation involving our different ministries or whatever.

I compare this to driving down the road; if we don't keep our eyes on the road ahead of us, we will crash. Think of it as the road to life, eternal life. We must keep our eyes on Jesus to keep from going off the road to Heaven.

First, we must realize when we are being distracted and pulled down by these thoughts. Our thoughts are not on Jesus. Or if we are watching others, how they look or how they act, we are not watching Jesus. When people gather around the altar, are you looking at them? Or are you looking at the ONE who made them?

Are you having thoughts and distractions like, "Boy is he ever a proud one; God should really deal with him." Or "I wonder if she's still seeing what's his name?"

Or even down to silly thoughts like, look at that dress she has on; she looks like she belongs on the street corner. Or now why doesn't she or he kneel when everyone else does? Or a few other thoughts one might have: she talks too much, he smells, boy she really aggravates me, their discernment is lacking, they are involved in evildoing, he is so lazy, she is so crazy!

46: KEEP YOUR EYES ON JESUS

Yes, we could say or think all of these things, but does God want us to? Remember the initials WWJD? <u>W</u>hat <u>W</u>ould <u>J</u>esus <u>D</u>o?

We must ask Jesus to help us see with HIS eyes, to see with His spiritual eyes, with the eyes of unconditional love, and know HE loves these people as much as He loves us. And to know to others WE are "these people!" Perhaps many are saying things about us too. So in either case we must "keep our eyes on Jesus." If they are talking about us, we need to look up to Jesus.

We must realize when we are not keeping our eyes on Him. We must ask Him to help us hold every thought captive. (Phil. 4:8) We need to think about what we are thinking about!

We must keep our eyes closed to the distractions of the world. Close our eyes during Mass and praise and worship HIM. He will handle all the battles to be fought. He will take care of it all, everything, even down to the finest detail.

If we are constantly fretting about others and what they are doing, we are off track. We are not keeping our eyes on Him.

Jesus loves each and every one of us right where we are! We used to sing a clown song about that. It goes like this: "Thank you, Lord, for giving us US times two. Thank You, Lord, for giving us <u>US</u> right where we are!"

Here are a few signs you are "off track." IF you have lost your peace, if you have gone off on a tangent, any time you are fearful, when you are overly involved with something that has you in constant turmoil. If you are constantly worried or fretful about something, if you are always "in a stew!"

So how do we deal with these thoughts and distractions? We must catch ourselves and ask are we thinking good thoughts, things of God? IF we have our eyes on Jesus, are we looking for the Jesus in others? Are we looking for the good in them and in ourselves? Or are we dwelling on the things not of God?

It always helps to put on some praise and worship music and let it permeate your thinking. Praise and worship always helps us stay focused on Him. HE dwells among our praises. We must ask God to change our way of thinking.

We must rise above the misery we are in and that of others if we are to FLY WITH THE EAGLES! He will lift us up as He says in Isiah 40:31. Reading scripture is another way to stay focused on HIM.

It all boils down to this: TRUST IN HIM and NOT in yourself. Give each situation to HIM and TRUST HE knows what you need, HE knows what HE is doing. His ways are not our ways. (Isaiah 55:8-9) Repeat after me.... "Jesus I trust in YOU, times three, then "Thy will be done!" times three! AMEN!

We must give every problem, however big or small, to Him. We must ask for an increase in faith and believe HE knows what is best for each one of us. He will handle every situation IF we let HIM! We must give every situation to Him in prayer. Proverbs 3:5-6 says, "Trust in the Lord with all your heart and lean NOT on your own

46: KEEP YOUR EYES ON JESUS

understanding. And in all your ways acknowledge HIM and HE will make your paths straight!"

He will guide you and lead you/us all the way to HEAVEN! AMEN!

"I pray I will make it to Heaven and be a saint (notice it is a lower case s). Lord have mercy on me, a sinner."

47

HOLINESS

A talk for intercessory prayer night. Aug. 9th, 2000

Matthew 5:48 says, "Be you therefore perfect, as also your Heavenly Father is perfect."

Are you perfect? I certainly am NOT!

Pope John Paul II called us to holiness, our priests call us to holiness, many of us have given talks on holiness. Everywhere we look we are being "called to holiness." And now, here is one more talk on holiness. First of all, we must give all thanksgiving to God, for HE is the One putting this desire to grow in holiness into our heart and on our minds. For it is only by God's grace we have this desire to achieve perfection. I thought instead of telling you we are all "called to holiness" maybe now it is time to help you and give some practical advice from one of the doctors of the Church.

St. Alphonsus of Liguori was a Bishop and Founder of the Redemptorists and a doctor of the Church. First a little about him, he was born in 1696 in Italy. He had a doctorate in both canon law and civil law at the age of sixteen, and

47: HOLINESS

he practiced law very successfully for eight years. But he abandoned the practice of law to become a priest and was ordained in 1726.

In 1732 he founded the Congregations of the Most Holy Redeemer, the Redemptorists. They have become famous for giving missions to enkindle and rejuvenate souls with true religious fervor. So let us all call upon him to intercede for us before we begin.

As many have said before, the first step in holiness is to spend time with Jesus. That "one on one" time with Him, where you give yourself completely to Him and sit in silence. Spend time before the Blessed Sacrament daily, or if your Church does not have the Blessed Sacrament exposed, then you can go to any Catholic Church and sit before the tabernacle. See Jesus with the eyes of faith. This practice is highly recommended by the masters of the spiritual life, and it brings good results. The Mass is a great help in spiritual growth. Mass is HEAVEN on Earth.

A few weeks ago, we heard one of our priests talk about the VIRTUES and how he had gone to the library and gotten out a book on Virtues that was very thick. He told us of how in religious orders they choose a different virtue every week or month, and then they concentrate on practicing that virtue for a set length of time. This practice is highly recommended by the masters of the spiritual life, and it brings good results.

Our first virtue to "work" on is FAITH! "I am the light of the World; he that follows me, walks not in darkness, but shall have the light of life." (John 8:12)

Faith is a divinely infused virtue by which man believes what God has revealed and teaches through His Holy Church. St. Paul calls faith "the substance of things to be hoped for, and the evidence of things that appear not. (Hebrews 11:1) Blessed are they that have not seen and have yet believed." (John 20:29)

Faith is a shield of protection against the enemies of our salvation. Our faith is a great gift, and without faith, hope could not exist.

Faith gives us a great means of showing our reverence and respect for God. We give glory to God, even when we can't see Him or understand Him. When we believe in Him, even though we cannot see Him or understand Him. "Blessed are they that have not seen and have believed." (John 20:29)

FAITH is also a shield of protection against the enemies of our salvation. St. John says: "This is the victory which overcometh the world, our faith." (1 John 5:3.) "This is the will of God; our sanctification" says the Apostle. (1 Thess. 4:3)

Remember my last talk when I spoke of the most important moment of our life is our death? Our lives should be lived for the purpose of our sanctification, for our salvation, and for the salvation of others. According to Holy Scripture in James 2:17, "Faith without works is dead." If we don't live our faith daily and believe daily, then we are dead spiritually. "Blessed are the poor in spirit for theirs is the Kingdom of Heaven." Matthew 5:3 If we are "poor in spirit," we are continually turning to God to ask for His help in our daily walk. We believe in Him.

47: HOLINESS

"Faith," says St. Augustine, "is characteristic not of the proud but of the humble." He who is truly humble never finds it hard to believe. We must have humble simplicity seen in the little child. TRUST IN GOD!

Oftentimes we are attacked by Satan with temptations to reject our faith; lift this temptation up to Jesus. Use the HOLY NAME OF JESUS to fight this temptation. Remember the song "In The Name of Jesus We Have the VICTORY!" We must pray, "Lord increase our faith." Luke 17:5. When attacked by Satan and we turn to Jesus, it becomes a great source of merit for us. Remember everything happening to us is first allowed by God. It doesn't mean He caused it, but He allowed it for a reason and a purpose. We may not know the reason or the purpose, but we must believe HE will turn it all to good at some point in our lives. God sees with far clearer eyes, He "sees" what is needed in our lives to bring us to salvation. Satan has many evil things planned for us, but Jesus turns them around for the good to those who LOVE the Lord. (Romans 8:28)

PRAY and ask God to increase your faith, HE WILL. Have faith to believe HE WILL. And do not be afraid of the way in which he chooses to increase your faith. Have EXPECTANT FAITH, or what I like to call PREGNANT FAITH! Expect God to work in your life and He will.

The Catechism of the Catholic Church says "faith is a theological virtue by which we believe in God and believe all that HE has said and revealed to us, and that Holy Church proposes for our belief, because HE is truth itself. By FAITH man freely commits his entire self to God. The believer seeks to know and to do God's will. The righteous shall live by faith." (CCC Faith: 26, 142, 150, 1814, 2087)

The gift of faith remains in one who has not sinned against it. But "faith apart from works is dead." When faith is deprived of hope and love, it does not fully unite the believer to Christ and does not make him a living member of His Body. Service of and witness to the faith are necessary for salvation: "So everyone who acknowledges Me before men, I also will acknowledge before My Father who is in Heaven, but whoever denies Me before men, I also will deny before My Father who is in Heaven." (Matthew 10:32)

Faith is instilled by God, but we resist it by our sins. We resist it by not "walking by faith." Anything causing us to be "out of God's grace" deceases our faith. We must guard our faith and be ever vigilant against those thoughts leading us away from God.

To me, Faith is a priceless jewel; for without faith, we do not come to know and to believe in Jesus. He calls us unceasingly all our lives; are we listening? Every Mass we attend should bring us that much closer to Heaven. That much closer to Jesus. We must examine our lives daily and ask God to show us where we have failed to see Him each day. Did we fail to see Him in the eyes of the poor? In the eyes of the lonely, the hurt, or the depressed? Did you see Jesus today? Did you see HIM in the eyes of our priests? Or in the homily of the priest? We see Him in the Most Holy Eucharist at every Mass or in Adoration. Did you see Him in the eyes of your children, your spouse, your coworkers?

47: HOLINESS

We must "see" with the eyes of our FAITH. It is a virtue practiced "moment by moment" throughout the day. If we ask God to show us with HIS EYES what HE wants or HOW HE wants us to see each situation, our faith will increase. As we read His Holy Word, our faith will increase. Spend some time reading scripture daily, and your faith will increase. This is probably why our priests are obligated to pray the Liturgy of the Hours several times a day. The Secular Franciscans are also asked to do this, at least morning and evening prayers, but it is not a sin if we are not able to do so each day.

Remember the words I heard the night I entered the Catholic Church? "Welcome into My Kingdom in a new and more POWERFUL way, my little clown, I have 'called' you to help rebuild My Church." It is hard for me to believe sometimes He wants to use little ole me, a little farm girl from the "boonies." But if He can use me, he can use anyone. He wants to use each one of us to "Help rebuild His Church!" YES, HE wants to use YOU too. FAITH is the gift He wishes to give to each and every one of us. The FAITH to believe in Him. To believe HE will take care of us and lead us on the straight and narrow road to our Salvation, where we will rejoice with Him together in Heaven one day. AMEN!

48

THE EUCHARIST A TALK GIVEN TO THE YOUTH ON DEC. 10, 2002

WOW! Where do I begin? The Eucharist is such an immense topic I cannot do it justice in a fifteen-minute talk. I have had a most difficult time knowing what to cover to try to hit the highlights in fifteen minutes. I think I will begin by saying the word Eucharist means thanksgiving (CCC 1322-1419).

Jesus Himself instituted the Most Holy Eucharist at His first Holy Mass on Holy Thursday, at the Last Supper. The Holy Eucharist is the third sacrament of initiation. It is a sacramental sacrifice of thanksgiving and praise. The Eucharist makes present the sacrifice of the cross in an unbloody manner. The sacrifice of Christ and the sacrifice of the Eucharist are one, single sacrifice. In the Eucharistic sacrifice of the cross, there is one priest and one victim: Christ.

48: THE EUCHARIST A TALK GIVEN

I think my efforts tonight will be directed toward helping you believe Jesus is truly present, Body, Blood, Soul, and Divinity, in the Most Holy Sacrifice of the Altar. And I know only the Holy Spirit will help you believe, and so I begin by asking the Holy Spirit to enlighten your hearts and minds as I share my testimony and the stories of Eucharistic Miracles. I pray HE will show you the truth of the Most Holy Eucharist.

First, we must "walk by faith and not by sight." We must have the faith to believe what Jesus tells us is the Truth in the Bible. It is very important we know our faith; if we know our faith and believe our faith, there is no way we could ever leave our faith or our Catholic Church. Many leave the Church because they do not know the true teachings of our Catholic Church. Polls have shown 70 percent of Catholics do not believe the Eucharist is the TRUE Body, Blood, Soul, and Divinity of Our Lord Jesus. We must pray for all to believe.

Do any of you know anyone who has left the Church because of all the scandals? I do. Whenever they tell me they have left the Church, the first question I ask is this; "Do you believe that Jesus is present in the Most Holy Eucharist?"

They did not believe the teachings of the Church. For if they truly believed Jesus is present Body, Blood, Soul, and Divinity as the Catholic Church teaches, how could anyone leave? If you leave, you are leaving Jesus in the Most Holy Eucharist.

Allow me to share a little of my testimony with you. First, I am a convert to Catholicism; no one "made me do it!" I was raised a Baptist, then as I got older, I attended a few non-denominational Churches where they always liked to bash the Catholics. In fact, many in their congregations were ex-Catholics. I wondered how they could always speak so negatively about another Church and say such mean things if they are Christians.

As for myself, I wouldn't even take the time to study and search the scriptures for the answers. I wanted HIM to tell me HIMSELF! This is called PRIDE, with a capital P! For, you see, I had always believed the Catholics were all going to Hell. That is how stubborn and prideful I was. When I finally decided to ask HIM, I gave Him "my will." You see, God is a Gentleman, and HE will never force you to do anything. You have free will, the will to say "YES" to Him or "NO" to Him. Well, I finally swallowed my pride and decided I would ask HIM what He wanted me to do. So, one time, at a Monday night prayer meeting, I asked Him, "Lord what would you have me to do? Show me, Lord; tell me, Lord." I begged Him to show me the TRUTH, is the Catholic Church where you would have me to be? Not what I want, but what do YOU want? Do you want me to become a Catholic?

And then I had what I call a "movie in my mind," and this is what I "saw." I will tell you the whole thing first, then I will explain it to you because as I was seeing it, I did not get the meaning of it until it was completed, then it all came to me in an instant.

I saw a huge fish, tail to the ceiling, head to the floor, about eight feet tall. As I watched this fish, I saw the scales

48: THE EUCHARIST A TALK GIVEN

begin to fall off of it. The scales fell onto the floor in a pile. Then behind the scales was pure white meat. As I looked at this white meat, it suddenly opened to reveal a crucifix deep inside! Jesus was on the Cross. WOW!

As soon as it was over, this is the meaning I received in an instant: the fish represented the Catholic Church. God has a sense of humor, as my father always used to call the Catholics "mackerel snatchers" because, in his day, they always ate fish on Fridays. Mackerel is a type of fish. Next the scales fell off onto the floor, this represented all the "garbage" I had always heard about the Church, all the junk I had heard. This was all falling to the ground. It also represented the scales falling off my eyes so I could see the truth. Behind the scales was pure white meat. This means that to find the truth we must dig deep, we must look for the truth, we must go beneath the surface, beneath what we have heard from others, and we need to look for ourselves. We need to study and read the *Lives of the Saints* and pray to God to show us the truth. The white meat meant purity and TRUTH.

Next, the meat opened and deep within was the Crucifix. The Catholic Church is the only Church that has Jesus on the Cross. The Protestants do not. When I saw this, I knew God led me to the One True Church, the Catholic Church. My first thought was, "Oh NOOOOOOOOOOOOOO!"

But because I knew what I had prayed, I had to listen to HIM and do what HE called me to do. So, I had to obey!

The next step was beginning the RCIA (Rite of Christian Initiation of Adults) process. This is where you learn about the Catholic Church teachings and decide if this is truly what you want to do. I had a very difficult time in RCIA. (The name has since been changed to OCIA by the United States Conference of Catholic Bishops. It now means Order of Christian Initiation for Adults.)

The class was a real "cross" for me. My "sponsor" was a very rotund guy, and he stood in the doorway of the room. A sponsor is only required to attend once a month, but my sponsor knew I would run if he wasn't blocking the door with his very big belly and his arms crossed. I couldn't get away! Then after each class, he would spend time explaining everything to make it clear what we had just covered in class.

After several months passed, it was time to go to Miami to the Cathedral to meet the Bishop. It is called the Rite of Sending. This was the same weekend of our yearly "Rally." The priest leading it told us if we had any problems or needed prayer, to ask the person seated next to you to pray for you. Well, I was in a predicament as I was supposed to go to meet the Bishop the next morning. I did not want to go because I was having trouble believing Jesus was truly ALIVE in the Eucharist. I did not want to be a hypocrite, so I did not want to go. So I explained this to the man sitting next to me, a complete stranger! He prayed over me, and I do not remember one thing he prayed. I went home and went to bed.

About 5 a.m. I awoke with a dream still fresh on my mind. I saw an oval-shaped bowl with water in it. Floating in the water appeared to be something looking like a

48: THE EUCHARIST A TALK GIVEN

ravioli; it was white, and it had substance to it. I could see it beating: thump, thump; thump, thump; thump, thump! As I watched, the bowl broke open and all the water came flowing down onto a table; the "ravioli" broke into many pieces all on the table. Each piece was still beating individually, and collectively they all formed the shape of a heart, with each piece. THEN I saw a dark-skinned, hairy arm come down from Heaven and pick up each piece and give it to the person who came forward. It was still beating as they received it.

Now for the meaning of the dream. The HOST was floating in a bowl of water, the LIVING WATER OF CHRIST. The "ravioli" was to show me there was substance in the Host, and it was beating, meaning HE is ALIVE in the EUCHARIST! As the bowl broke open, the living water of Christ came down to cleanse the people. The Host broke into many pieces, all still beating. Which means HE IS ALIVE in each Host, and HE is still complete in each one. All the pieces together on the altar formed a huge heart, the heart of Jesus! The dark-skinned, hairy arm coming down from Heaven was Jesus, and the priest is in persona Christi, as he serves the people of God. Each Host is complete. And whole and ALIVE!!! Praise God! I finally believed the Eucharist is the TRUE BODY, BLOOD, SOUL, AND DIVINITY of our LORD and SAVIOR, Jesus Christ! AMEN! Just in time for me to go to Miami and meet the Bishop that very same morning. Now you understand why I did not want to go originally, because I did not want to be a hypocrite, but NOW I BELIEVED, and I still do! My story is almost unbelievable, but I know I had to share it as it might help someone else come to know our Lord in the Most Holy Eucharist. If they think I am crazy, they are right.... I am CRAZY for our Lord and Savior, Jesus Christ! AMEN! I don't worry about what others will think.

49
EUCHARISTIC MIRACLES

One day St. Anthony of Padua was challenged by a rich Jewish man. He said to St. Anthony, "I do not believe that the Eucharist is Jesus. Prove it! I will take my donkey and put him in the town square, I will starve him for three days, and then I will put a big pile of hay out for him at a distance. You put your Eucharist out for him, and we shall see what he does, if he goes to my hay or to the Eucharist."

Saint Anthony was put on the spot, and so he accepted the challenge. Then for the next three days, he fasted and prayed in a nearby Church. On the third day, the man released his donkey, and he made a bee line straight for the hay. Just before reaching it, St. Anthony stepped out in front of him with an elevated Host, saying, "STOP, donkey, and adore your Christ." Immediately the donkey dropped his front legs to the ground, in a position of adoration, and bowed down to the Eucharist in adoration. The rich Jew was changed on the spot and converted to Catholicism. And he paid for a Church to be built on that spot, with a picture of the event carved on the cornerstone. It is still in existence today. Praise God!

Now think about that; is a donkey smarter than you are? If we do not truly believe, are we dumber than that donkey? Think about it, pray about it and ask GOD to show you. This is a very personal thing and is between you and God. Tonight, we will be praying over you to truly believe, IF you are willing to say "YES" to God. Those who already do believe can receive prayer for an increase in their faith. Those who do not believe can ask HIM themselves, and we will pray and ask God to reveal the TRUTH to you. You must be willing to surrender to God; that is all. HE WILL DO THE REST. Give HIM your will and let HIM show you the truth. You do not have to take my word for it. We will ask the HOLY SPIRIT to convict and convince your heart and minds to the truth. If you still have trouble believing, just keep praying every day, and HE will give you the faith you need to truly believe. It might not be immediate, it might not be tonight, but HE will help you believe.

A Prayer:

Help us Lord Jesus, to truly believe in Your Presence, Body, Blood, Soul, and Divinity in Your Most Holy Sacrament of the Altar, the Holy Eucharist. The word Eucharist means thanksgiving, help us to always give thanks to You, Lord, for always being with us, for "giving us this day our daily bread" at daily Mass. Thank You for humbling Yourself and coming to us at each Mass, to renew us, purify us, strengthen us, and heal us. Thank You for coming into union with us, for living in us, for helping

49: EUCHARISTIC MIRACLES

us to "be Eucharist" to "be Jesus" for and to others. Thank You for the "Jesus that lives within us," thank You for transforming our lives and using us to help others. Amen and Amen!

50

SCRIPTURAL BASIS OF THE EUCHARIST

"And Melchizedek King of Salem brought out bread and wine, he was priest of God Most High." (Genesis 14:18)

"Do not labor for the food which perishes, but for the food which endures to eternal life, which the Son of man will give to you; for on Him has God the Father set His seal." (John 6:27)

"I am the bread of life; he who comes to me shall not hunger and he who believes in me shall never thirst." (John 6:35)

"I am the living bread which came down from Heaven; if anyone eats of this bread, he will live forever and the bread which I shall give for the life of the world is MY flesh." (John 6:51)

"Truly, truly, I say to you, unless you eat the flesh of the Son of man and drink His blood, you will have no life in you; he who eats My flesh and drinks My blood has eternal life, and I will raise him up on the last day." (John 6:53-56)

50: SCRIPTURAL BASIS

Many of those who heard Jesus say this couldn't accept it despite the fact HE explained and further clarified His statements three times in attempting to address their lack of understanding and their unwillingness to accept His words. He tried again a fourth time to help them comprehend what He said.

"It is the spirit that gives life, the flesh is of no avail; the words that I have spoken to you are spirit and life." (John 6:63)

After saying this, many of those who had been following Him chose to stay away. He tried four times to teach them, and in the end, only a few accepted His teachings.

Now as they were eating, Jesus took bread and blessed and broke it, and gave it to the disciples and said, "Take, eat; THIS IS MY BODY." And HE took the cup, and when He had given thanks, HE gave it to them, saying, "Drink of it, all of you; for THIS IS MY BLOOD OF THE COVENANT, WHICH IS POURED OUT FOR THE MANY FOR THE FORGIVENES OF SINS" (Matthew 26:26-28).

Clearly Jesus said HE was giving His followers His Body and Blood. It wasn't meant as a symbol as many of His followers would have liked to believe; it was totally HIM.

"Whoever, therefore, eats the bread or drinks the cup of the Lord in an unworthy manner will be guilty of profaning the Body and Blood of the Lord. Let a man examine himself, and so eat of the bread and drink of the cup. For anyone who eats and drinks without discerning the Body eats and drinks judgment upon himself." (1 Corinthians 11:27-29)

The Eucharist is Christ's sacrifice made present in every Mass.

(Note: if you want to learn more about the Eucharist, you can read in the Catechism of the Catholic Church numbers 1322–1419.)

51
OUR LIVES ARE LIKE A STREAM IN THE DESERT (LV)

We start at the top of the stream, and suddenly life narrows the stream and puts some pressure on us. God squeezes us and "puts the pressure on." Something catastrophe happens in our lives: sickness, sadness, tragedy, loss, even death of a loved one. So we are deep in the stream running through the desert. We cry out to the Lord, and we turn to Him. We give our lives to Him and beg HIM to help us. "Please Lord, HELP! Do not let us drown in this stream." Then the stream begins to flow slowly for a while; the bank of the river holds us safely in God's hands. Then do we stay close to God? Or do we become apathetic and lazy?

"Oh no! What is that huge boulder doing in my stream?" It's in our way: an obstacle, perhaps things aren't going the way we had planned. What about God's plan? He helps us to go around the obstacles in our lives, the boulders in our way, if we allow Him to guide us.

Or do we think we can do this on our own? When we try to do it on our own, we hit the rock with a thud! OUCH! Pain hits, emotional and physical. Rough waters slam us up against that hard rock. "It hurts, Lord; why me, Lord? I've been good." Whine away, dear heart, whine away, but turn to God once again. He will steer us around the huge boulders and the little rocks in our way in the middle of our stream, or He will help us over them.

And so we float downstream, gently rolling on. Little rocks enter our path again, but now we have begun to learn these rocks are here for a greater purpose; to mold us and make us more understanding of others' pain. OUCH, Yes, they hurt, but HE brings us His comfort in our own pain. We are growing closer and closer to Him.

The desert is dry and dark and cold at night. It is a very long night sometimes, but He is there with us. We are NOT alone. The long cold night brings fear of "what goes bump in the night." Be of good COURAGE, FEAR NOT He tells us. Be still and listen to His still small voice within us in the desert.

52

"GRAMMA ROSA" THE POWER OF PRAYER, EVEN IN THE LITTLE THINGS

This book would not be complete if I did not share a story about "Gramma Rosa" (RIP). She was a little old Italian lady at our Church in Florida, and whenever we had a festival coming up, she would start praying ahead of time we would have good weather. And we always had no rain, year after year. So after she had passed to her eternal life, I asked her to intercede to God for me whenever I needed it to stop raining, even if only for a few minutes.

One night a priest and I sat on a bench outside the Church office waiting for the rain to stop so we could walk to the Chapel without getting wet. The rain was very heavy, and it was raining sideways as the wind blew! I said to him, "Watch this," and I prayed a short prayer asking Gramma Rosa, through our Lord, to have it stop raining just long enough for us to get to the chapel without getting wet. Within a few seconds after praying this prayer, the rain STOPPED completely! The priest said to me, "She's a saint!" We laughed and off we went to the Chapel without getting a drop of rain on us!

Another time my husband and I drove in the rain, and we were almost at the farm where I grew up. I asked Gramma Rosa to pray to our Lord for it to stop raining just long enough for us to get into the cabin with our suitcases without getting wet. About two minutes before arriving at the cabin, it stopped raining. And there was a beautiful rainbow out over the meadow touching the earth as we came down the hill. Once again, Gramma Rosa "pulled through" for us. Over the years there have been many other times I have asked her to make it stop raining just for a few minutes, and she has never failed this prayer! Try it yourself, and see if she helps you. I think she is the future Saint of stopping rainy weather, even if just for a few minutes!

Asking someone to pray for us, whether they are on Earth or have already passed on, is good. Catholics believe in the Communion of Saints, and it is OK to ask them to pray to Jesus on our behalf.

However, It is NOT OK to try to "contact" them or ask them questions as this opens you up to the evil one. Be careful!

53

SOME DAILY PRAYERS YOU MIGHT LIKE

We should ask for the light to see the will of God, and you must ask for the courage to be able to do the will of God."
—Venerable Msgr. Aloysius Schwartz

A daily prayer of St. Francis of Assisi:
Lord, help me to live this day, quietly, easily.
To lean upon Thy great strength, trustfully, restfully.
To wait for the unfolding of Thy will, patiently, serenely.
To meet others, peacefully, joyously.
To face tomorrow, confidently, courageously.
Amen
Daily Morning Prayer of Saint Francis of Assisi.

Jesus Lord, I offer You this new day because I believe in You, love You, hope all things in You and thank You for Your blessings. I am sorry for having offended You and forgive everyone who has offended me. Lord, look on me and leave in me peace and courage and Your humble wisdom that I may serve others with JOY, and be pleasing to You all day. Amen.

A favorite quote of St. Francis of Assisi

"Start by doing what is necessary. Then do what is possible. Suddenly you will be doing the impossible.

Another beautiful prayer is the Franciscan Crown Rosary, Secular Franciscans are encouraged to pray this on Saturdays.

Some prayers that I pray from the heart:

> Jesus, I trust in You, Jesus, I trust in You, Jesus, I trust in You,
> Thy will be done, Thy will be done, Thy will be done.
> Lord, please heal me mentally, physically, emotionally, and spiritually,
> the most important being spiritually. Amen
> Lord have mercy, Christ have mercy, Lord have mercy. Amen

Other beautiful prayers: The Rosary, the Our Father, The Glory, Franciscan Crown Rosary, Guardian angel prayer, Prayer to St. Michael the Archangel, The Chaplet of Divine Mercy and also prayers from your heart.

53: SOME DAILY PRAYERS

Your Cross

The everlasting God has in His wisdom foreseen from eternity the cross that He now presents to you as a gift from His inmost Heart. This cross He now sends you He has considered with His all-knowing eyes, understood with His Divine mind, tested with His wise justice, warmed with loving arms, and weighed with His own hands to see that it be not one inch too large and not one ounce too heavy for you. He has blessed it with His Holy Name, anointed it with His grace, perfumed it with His consolation, taken one last look at you and your courage, and then sent it to you from Heaven, a special greeting from God to you, alms of the all-merciful love of God.
—St. Francis de Sales
"I've talked the talk Lord, now help me to walk the walk. HELP ME to practice what I preach!" Amen. (LV)
Lesley Mason Vaitekunas OFS, Author

1. Lesley with Auntie Francies's 1927 Model A in the background.

2. Lesley and her brother "having tea."

3. Lesley May age 5 with a neighbors horse.

4. Lesley May about age 3.